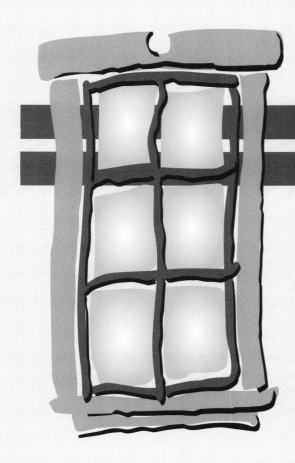

MICROSOFT
WINDOWS NT 4.0

A TUTORIAL
TO ACCOMPANY
PETER NORTON'S
INTRODUCTION
TO COMPUTERS

GLENCOE
McGraw-Hill

New York, New York   Columbus, Ohio   Woodland Hills, California   Peoria, Illinois

Microsoft Windows NT 4.0
A Tutorial to Accompany
Peter Norton's Introduction to Computers

Glencoe/McGraw-Hill

A Division of The **McGraw·Hill** Companies

Send all inquiries to:
Glencoe/McGraw-Hill
936 Eastwind Drive
Westerville, OH 43081

ISBN 0-02-804359-6

Development: FSCreations, Inc.
Production: MicroPublishing

Windows NT, Windows 95, Office 97, Word, Word for Windows, Word 6, WordPad, NotePad, Microsoft Works, MS-DOS, OLE 2.0, and *OLE 1.0* are trademarks of Microsoft Corporation.

Lotus 1-2-3 and *LotusWorks* are trademarks of Lotus Development Corporation.

ClarisWorks is a registered trademark of Claris Corporation.

dBASE is a trademark of Borland Corporation.

1 2 3 4 5 6 7 8 9   083   02 01 00 99 98 97

CONTENTS

LESSON 4
EXPLORING DISK ORGANIZATION   **7 4**

LESSON 5
MANAGING YOUR FILES   98

LESSON 6
WINDOWS NT ACCESSORIES   124

LESSON 7
CONTROLLING PRINTING FEATURES   **154**

LESSON 8
COPYING, MOVING, EXCHANGING, AND SHARING DATA   172

COMMAND SUMMARY   191

GLOSSARY   203

INDEX   211

PREFACE

Microsoft Windows NT Tutorial, one of the instructional tools that complements Peter Norton's *Introduction to Computers,* covers the basic features of Windows NT (version 4.0). Glencoe and Peter Norton have teamed up to provide this tutorial and its ancillaries to help you become a knowledgeable, empowered end user. After you complete this tutorial, you will be able to explain the concepts of this operating system.

STRUCTURE AND FORMAT OF THE WINDOWS NT TUTORIAL

Microsoft Windows NT Tutorial covers a range of functions and techniques and provides hands-on opportunities for you to practice and apply your skills. Each lesson in *Microsoft Windows NT Tutorial* includes the following:

■ *Contents and Objectives.* The Contents and Objectives provide an overview of the Windows NT features you will learn in the lesson.

■ *Explanations of important concepts.* Each section of each lesson begins with a brief explanation of the concept or software feature covered in that lesson. The explanations help you understand "the big picture" as you learn each new Windows NT feature.

■ *New terms.* An important part of learning about computers is learning the terminology. Each new term in the tutorial appears in boldface, is defined the first time it is used, and appears in the margin. As you encounter these words, read their definitions carefully. If you encounter the same word later and have forgotten its meaning, you can look up the word in the Glossary.

■ *Hands On activities.* Because most of us learn best by doing, each explanation is followed by a hands-on activity that includes step-by-step instructions, which you complete at the computer. Integrated in the steps are notes, tips, and warnings to help you learn Windows NT.

■ *Illustrations.* Many figures point out features on the screen and illustrate what your screen should look like after you complete important steps.

■ *Lesson Summary.* At the end of each lesson, a Lesson Summary reviews the major topics covered in the lesson. You can use the Lesson Summary as a study guide.

■ *New Terms to Remember.* All the new terms introduced in the lesson are identified. Verify that you can define each term.

■ *Review exercises.* At the end of each lesson are three types of objective questions: a Matching Exercise, a Completion Exercise, and Short-Answer Questions. When you complete these exercises, you can verify that you have learned all the concepts and skills that have been covered in the lesson.

- *Application Projects.* The Application Projects provide additional hands-on practice to apply your problem-solving skills and your skills to use Windows NT.
- *Command Summary, Glossary, and Index.* A Command Summary, a Glossary, and an Index appear at the back of the tutorial. Use the Command Summary as a reference for specific commands and shortcuts. Toolbar buttons are included where appropriate. Use the Glossary to look up terms that you don't understand and the Index to find specific information.
- *Student Data Disk.* Attached to the inside back cover of this tutorial you will find a 3½" disk called the Student Data Disk. This disk contains Windows NT files for you to use as you complete the hands-on activities and the end-of-lesson activities. Before you use the Student Data Disk, make a backup copy immediately. If you run out of storage space as you use your Student Data Disk to complete the activities in this tutorial, save additional files to a blank formatted disk.

After you complete this tutorial, you will have the skills necessary to create, process, and present information in a variety of ways using Windows NT, thus helping you to become a highly productive employee in today's workforce.

ABOUT PETER NORTON

Peter Norton is a pioneering software developer and an author. Norton's Desktop for Windows, Utilities, Backup, AntiVirus and other utility programs are installed worldwide on millions of personal computers. His *Inside the IBM PC* and *DOS Guide* have helped countless individuals understand computers from the inside out.

Glencoe teamed up with Peter Norton to help you better understand the role computers play in your life now and in the future. As you begin to work in your chosen profession, you may use this tutorial now and later as a reference book.

REVIEWERS

Many thanks are due to Larry Manning, Tyler Junior College, Tyler, Texas, and Nancy Collins, ECPI College of Technology, Virginia Beach, Virginia, who reviewed the manuscript and provided recommendations to improve the tutorial.

MICROSOFT

WINDOWS NT 4.0

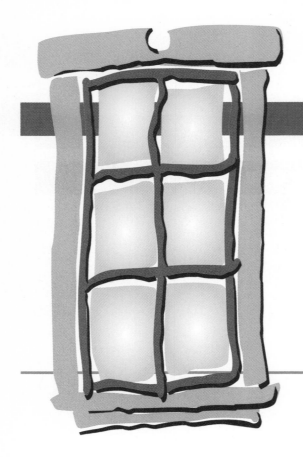

LESSON 1

EXPLORING

THE WINDOWS NT 4.0

DESKTOP

OBJECTIVES

After you complete this lesson, you will be able to do the following:

- *Describe what an operating system does.*

- *Boot your computer system.*

- *Identify the elements on your Windows NT 4.0 Desktop.*

- *Use your mouse to point, click, double-click, drag, and call up shortcut menus.*

- *Activate Desktop icons.*

- *Recognize the components of a dialog box.*

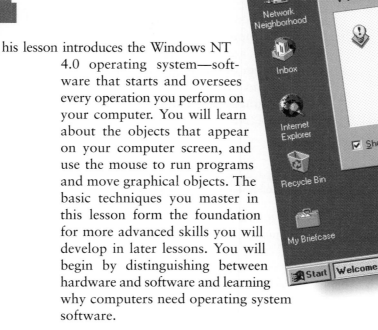

This lesson introduces the Windows NT 4.0 operating system—software that starts and oversees every operation you perform on your computer. You will learn about the objects that appear on your computer screen, and use the mouse to run programs and move graphical objects. The basic techniques you master in this lesson form the foundation for more advanced skills you will develop in later lessons. You will begin by distinguishing between hardware and software and learning why computers need operating system software.

INTRODUCING OPERATING SYSTEM SOFTWARE

hardware The parts of a computer system that you can see and touch.

software A collective term for programs, the instructions that are stored in electronic form and tell the computer what to do.

application Specialized software program for accomplishing a specific task, such as creating text, manipulating financial information, or keeping track of records.

operating system (software) A collection of programs that allows you to work with a computer by managing the flow of data between input devices, the computer's memory, storage devices, and output devices.

commands Instructions that you issue to the computer, usually by choosing from a menu, clicking a button, or pressing a combination of keys on the keyboard.

The computer system you work with consists of hardware and software. Usually, the **hardware** includes:

- A *processor* to manage, interpret, and manipulate the flow of data
- A *keyboard* to type information
- A *mouse* (or trackball) to point to objects and select options on the screen
- A *monitor* to see what you are doing
- A *printer* to produce hard copy output
- *Disks* to store information

Your computer system also needs both task-specific and general operational **software**. Software that helps you accomplish a specific task is called an **application**. You might use an application to type a letter, manage a budget, balance a checkbook, or organize a mailing list. Software that allows you to operate your hardware and use applications is called **operating system software**, or an **operating system** for short.

Sometimes the operating system manages your computer automatically. When you turn on your computer, the operating system looks up the current date and time, sets your preferred speaker volume, and displays the screen color scheme of your choice. At other times, your operating system follows your instructions, such as when you duplicate a specific file or launch a particular application. These computer instructions are called **commands**.

Not all personal computers use the same operating system software. Your computer's operating system determines not only the specific commands your system can execute but also the manner in which you give those commands and otherwise interact with your computer. This human-

user interface A term for the rules and methods by which a computer and its users communicate.

graphical user interface (GUI) An operating environment in which controls and data are visible on screen so they can be selected with a pointing device.

computer interaction is called the **user interface**. It determines the look and feel of your computing experience.

Microsoft's goal for Windows NT 4.0 is to create a pleasing, easy to use operating system that manages computer hardware and software more efficiently than previous operating systems. To meet these goals, Windows NT 4.0 utilizes a **graphical user interface** (or **GUI**), where you will use on-screen pictures to operate your computer. Let's get started!

STARTING THE COMPUTER WITH WINDOWS NT 4.0

Power On Self Test (POST) A program that checks a computer system's memory, keyboard, display, and disk drives.

booting the system, **system boot** Another expression for starting up, which the computer often accomplishes by loading a small program, which then reads a larger program into memory.

When you turn on the computer, a complex series of events begins. First, a built-in program tests the computer. This **Power On Self Test (POST)** checks the computer system memory, keyboard, display, and disk drives. Next, files from the hard disk containing essential operating system components are loaded. Because computer systems and setups vary greatly, you may see a series of screens informing you of the progress of the startup procedure. Finally, Windows NT displays its opening screen. Once you turn on the power, the computer gives itself the instructions it needs to start up or "pulls itself up by its bootstraps." From this figure of speech, the entire process is called **booting the system** or performing a **system boot**.

BOOTING WINDOWS NT

In the following steps, you will start the computer and boot the Windows NT operating system.

NOTE *If your computer is already on, you may need to restart your system. Check with your instructor, network administrator, or lab technician for details.*

 HANDS ON

1. Press the power button or flip the power switch to turn on the computer.

2. If the monitor connected to the system has a separate power switch, be sure to turn it on as well.

3. Observe the booting process.

   a. Listen for the POST sound. A single beep means the system passed all the tests; a series of beeps indicates a hardware problem. If you hear a series of beeps, check your keyboard and monitor connections, read the message on the screen, or consult your computer manual to fix the problem by yourself. You may need technical help from the manufacturer, a lab assistant, or a technician.

   b. Watch the screen. After a few moments, you see a memory indicator while the system checks its random access memory. Then some information appears at the top of the screen, followed by the Windows NT copyright screen as more of the operating system loads into memory. The Begin Logon screen appears next.

4. Press Ctrl + Alt + Delete simultaneously.

The Logon Information screen requests your user name and password.

log on The process of identifying yourself to the computer system. Logging on determines how the user may interact with the system, including the resources to which the user has access. Users can also set up the user interface to match their own needs and preferences.

user name A unique name generally assigned to the user by the network administrator.

password In Windows NT, a code (up to 14 characters) known only to the user. Having a secret password ensures that only authorized users can access the computer system.

window A rectangular area that displays information, such as the content of a document or the controls of an application; a window can be opened, closed, moved, sized, maximized, and minimized.

button A box labeled with words or pictures that can be clicked to select a setting or put a command into effect.

When you **log on** to a computer, you inform the operating system who you are. The operating system chooses your personal settings to complete the booting process. Systems that have multiple users, such as networks, keep track of who is allowed to access the computer by assigning unique **user names**. You may not be able to select your own user name; rather, a network administrator may assign the name to you. To provide security, each user must have a secret code known only to the user. In Windows NT, each user chooses a **password** (up to 14 characters) entered along with the user name during the logon procedure. When choosing a password, you should pick a series of letters, numbers, or special characters that would be difficult for someone else to guess. If you suspect that someone else knows your password, you should change your secret code immediately.

5. Type your user name.

6. Press Tab and type your password.

Asterisks appear as you type your password. In this way, others who may see your logon screen will not learn your password.

You may see the Welcome **window**, as shown in Figure 1-1. Windows are rectangular on-screen frames in which you do your computing work. Windows NT derives its name from these frames. The Welcome window displays *Did You Know...* plus a tip for using Windows NT. The Welcome window contains several **buttons**, sculpted boxes with words or pictures on them that execute commands. The Welcome window buttons allow you to view information about what is new in Windows NT, get help with Windows NT features, or display the next *Did You Know...*tip.

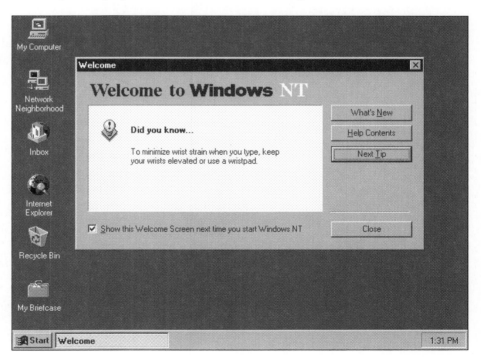

FIGURE 1-1

The Windows NT 4.0 Welcome window

7. If the Welcome dialog box appears, press Esc on your keyboard.

Desktop The working area of the screen which displays many Windows NT tools and is the background for your computer work.

Now your screen should resemble Figure 1-2. This screen, called the Windows NT **Desktop**, contains many of the tools for working with Windows NT and is the background for your computer work.

FIGURE 1-2

The Windows NT 4.0 Desktop

USING THE WINDOWS NT DESKTOP

In this section, you will learn the names and purposes of the objects on the Windows NT Desktop and perform useful tasks with them.

THE TASKBAR

taskbar An area on the Windows NT Desktop which displays buttons for the Start menu, Clock, and any open windows.

At the bottom of the screen is the **taskbar**, shown in Figure 1-3. In addition to containing the Start and Clock buttons, the taskbar displays buttons with the names of applications that are currently running. The taskbar lets you identify and choose among these programs. (In Figure 1-3, the standard Windows NT setup, the taskbar is at the bottom of the screen, and the Clock on the far right is the only running application). The Start button lets you locate and use additional applications.

NOTE   *You may see other objects on the taskbar in addition to the Clock, depending on the way your computer system is configured.*

FIGURE 1-3

The taskbar

DESKTOP ICONS

On the left side of your screen, you should see several small, labeled pictures, such as My Computer and Recycle Bin, as shown in Figure 1-4 (your

icon A small image that represents a device, program, file, or folder.

Desktop may include other icons). These pictures are called **icons**. Icons are graphical representations of objects such as programs, groups of programs, disk drives, documents, or specific tasks. Because icons are memorable, attractive, and easy to use, most Windows programs use icons.

FIGURE 1-4

Icons on the Desktop

The My Computer icon represents your computer system and lets you explore and manage it. The Recycle Bin allows you to delete and recover information. Because they help you manage your computer, these icons are called **system icons**. The other icons on your Desktop let you access other computers on your network or through your modem—features you will explore in later chapters. Each Desktop icon is a **shortcut icon**, a quick way to activate the program or task associated with it. Later, you will learn to make custom Desktop icons—shortcuts to the work you do most often on the computer, such as writing a memo, checking an appointments calendar, or managing your household budget.

system icon A picture representing an operating system file.

shortcut icon A picture representing a quick path to a program or task.

WINDOWS

open To access the contents of an icon in a window.

close To remove a window from the screen.

Icon contents can be displayed within a window. You **open** an icon to display its contents and **close** a window to remove it from the Desktop. You will open icons and close windows as you learn to use the mouse and manipulate windows more thoroughly in Lesson 2.

USING THE MOUSE

The mouse is used extensively in Windows NT. The mouse is the key to the graphical user interface because it lets you choose and manipulate on-screen objects without having to type on the keyboard.

POINTING

pointer (or **mouse pointer**)
An arrow or other on-screen image that moves in relation to the movement of a mouse or trackball.

pointing Moving the mouse pointer to position it over an on-screen object.

On your screen you should see an arrow pointing toward the upper-left. This arrow is called the **mouse pointer**, or more simply, the **pointer**. Moving the mouse on a horizontal surface moves the pointer around the screen. Move the mouse to the left or right, and the pointer moves to the left or right. Move the mouse away from you, and the pointer moves up the screen; move the mouse toward you, and the pointer moves down the screen.

Not surprisingly, this technique of positioning the pointer on the screen is called **pointing**. Pointing to particular objects on the screen or giving a particular command may change the shape of the pointer. When you must wait for the computer to accomplish a task, such as starting up Windows NT, an hourglass appears next to the arrow. Figure 1-5 shows several shapes you may notice as you point to objects on the screen.

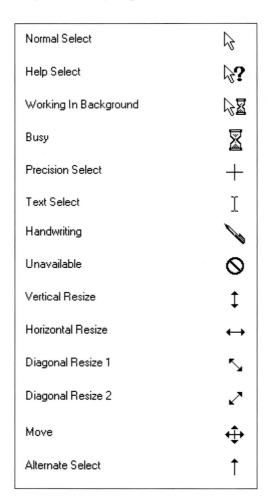

Normal Select	
Help Select	
Working In Background	
Busy	
Precision Select	
Text Select	
Handwriting	
Unavailable	
Vertical Resize	
Horizontal Resize	
Diagonal Resize 1	
Diagonal Resize 2	
Move	
Alternate Select	

FIGURE 1-5
Common pointer shapes

TIP   *FOR RIGHT-HANDED MOUSE USERS: Keep the mouse on the right side of the key-board. Cup the mouse in your hand so that the base of your palm or wrist rests on the desk while your index finger rests lightly on the left button. (See Figure 1-6.) Doing this lets you move and stop the mouse smoothly—the friction of your palm against the desk stops the mouse when you stop moving your hand.*

FIGURE 1-6

How to hold the mouse

T I P

FOR LEFT-HANDED USERS: To follow the right-handed instructions in this book, place the mouse on the left side of the keyboard and use your ring finger to click the left button.

After completing this book (and if you have your own computer), you may choose to switch your mouse button functions for ease of use. Windows NT lets you reassign the mouse buttons so that the right button performs the actions ordinarily performed by the left button.

CLICKING

clicking The technique of quickly pressing and releasing the left button on a mouse or trackball.

highlight To change the color of an object to one that contrasts with its usual appearance.

select To designate (typically by clicking an item with the mouse) where the next action will take place, which command will be executed next, or which option will be put into effect.

Pressing down a mouse button and releasing it is called **clicking** because of the sound the action makes. Although your mouse may have two or three buttons, you will use the left button most often. Thus clicking refers to the left mouse button, unless an instruction specifies a different button.

What happens when you click the mouse button depends upon the object your pointer is pointing to. Clicking a button on your screen activates its command; clicking an icon changes its color or **highlights** the icon. A highlighted icon is said to be chosen or **selected** so that you can act on it, such as by copying or deleting it. For this reason, Windows NT and other graphical user interfaces are referred to as "point and click" interfaces. Point and click software minimizes keyboarding.

N O T E

In this text, the verb "select" means to click something once with the left mouse button.

DOUBLE-CLICKING

double-click The technique of rapidly pressing and releasing the left button on a mouse or trackball twice when the mouse pointer on screen is pointing to an object.

To perform certain tasks, you must click the left mouse button twice in rapid succession without moving the pointer. This technique, called **double-clicking**, may require some practice. Clicking two times is not the same as double-clicking. It's a matter of timing. To assist in double-clicking, make sure your index finger is resting on the left button. Then, just "twitch" your index finger twice to double-click. Remember to rest the base of your palm or wrist on the desk so the mouse doesn't move.

DRAG-AND-DROP

drag-and-drop (or **dragging**) The technique of moving an object on screen by pointing to the object, pressing and holding the left mouse button, moving the mouse to the new location, and then releasing the button.

You can move many objects around the screen. To accomplish this task, you point to the object to be moved, press and hold the left button, move the mouse to drag the object to the desired location, and then release the mouse button. This series of actions is known as **drag-and-drop** or sometimes just **dragging**.

PRACTICING MOUSE TECHNIQUES

In the following steps, you will become familiar with using the mouse to select, open, and move objects on the Desktop.

HANDS ON

1. Point to the My Computer system icon. (Position the mouse pointer over this icon.)

2. Click My Computer. (Click the left mouse button to select the icon).

   Notice that the selected icon highlights (changes color).

3. To deselect the icon, position the pointer anywhere over the Desktop away from the system icon and click the left mouse button.

   The icon **deselects** or returns to its original color.

deselect To return an object to its original color or turn off an option, indicating that an item will not be affected by the next action you take or that an option will no longer be in effect.

4. Point to the My Computer icon.

5. Double-click (the left mouse button) to open the icon (display its contents).

   The My Computer window appears, as shown in Figure 1-7.

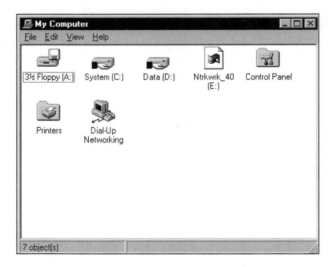

FIGURE 1-7

The My Computer window

6. Double-click the Control Panel folder.

The Control Panel window appears, as shown in Figure 1-8. It contains a series of icons that let you customize your computing environment.

Clicking a window's Close button—the X located in its upper-right corner—removes the window from the screen.

Close button

FIGURE 1-8
The Control Panel window

7. Click the Control Panel window's Close button.

The Control Panel window is removed from the Desktop.

8. Select the My Computer window's Close button.

The My Computer window is removed from the Desktop.

Next you'll drag-and-drop the My Computer icon to move it to a different location on the Desktop.

9. Point to the My Computer icon.

10. Press and hold the left mouse button while the pointer is over the icon. Move the mouse down and away from you to drag the icon from its current position to the lower-right corner of the screen. Then release the mouse button.

The icon should appear somewhere near the lower-right corner of the screen, as shown in Figure 1-9.

11. Use your mouse and the dragging technique to return the My Computer icon to its original location.

OPENING THE TASKBAR MENU

menu A list of items on the screen from which you can choose; menu usually refers to a list of commands or options.

A **menu** is a list of items on the screen from which you can choose. In the following steps, you will continue to practice using your mouse as you explore the function of the taskbar.

HANDS ON

1. Point to an empty part of the taskbar.

2. Click the *right* mouse button.

A menu for the taskbar appears, as shown in Figure 1-10.

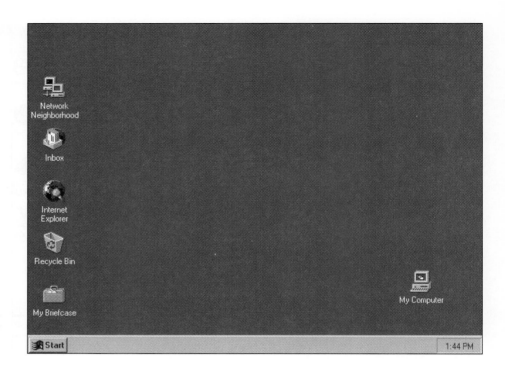

FIGURE 1-9
*The moved
My Computer icon*

FIGURE 1-10
The taskbar menu

3. In the menu, use the left mouse button to click Properties.

The Taskbar Properties dialog box appears. Notice that the set of Taskbar Options is visible, as shown in Figure 1-11.

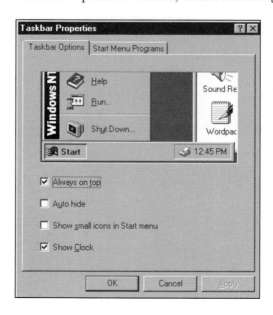

FIGURE 1-11
The Taskbar Options

4. Click the Close button for the Taskbar Properties dialog box.

The dialog box is removed from the Desktop.

OPENING THE START MENU

In the following steps, you will continue using the taskbar and mouse to open menus and select commands.

HANDS ON

1. Click the taskbar's Start button.

The Start menu appears, as shown in Figure 1-12.

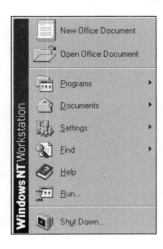

New Office Document
Open Office Document
Programs ▶
Documents ▶
Settings ▶
Find ▶
Help
Run...
Shut Down...

Windows NT Workstation

FIGURE 1-12
The Start menu

N O T E   *The Start menu on your computer may appear slightly different, depending on the way your computer system is configured.*

Notice the arrows next to many of the menu choices. These arrows indicate that menu choices contain additional menus or information.

2. Point to the Programs menu.

Another menu appears to the right of the first menu.

N O T E   *Pointing to a menu item without clicking highlights that item. Clicking the item chooses or activates it.*

3. Point to the Accessories menu.

Another menu appears.

4. Select (click with the left mouse button) WordPad.

N O T E   *From now on, when you must click a menu item with the left mouse button, you will be asked simply to select its name—for example, "Select WordPad," without the added instruction to "click with the left mouse button."*

The WordPad window appears on the Desktop. WordPad is a word processing accessory program that comes with the Windows NT operating system. You will learn more about using WordPad in Lesson 6.

5. Click the WordPad Close button.

The window is removed from the Desktop.

CLEARING MENUS

Sometimes you will want to clear menus without choosing one of their items. These steps show you how to clear unwanted menus from the Desktop.

HANDS ON

1. Click the Start menu.

A menu appears.

2. Point to Programs.

Another menu appears to the right of the first menu.

3. Point to Accessories.

N O T E   *The contents of your menus may differ significantly from those in the illustrations, depending on the way your computer system is configured.*

As Figure 1-13 shows, you now have a series of three menus displayed.

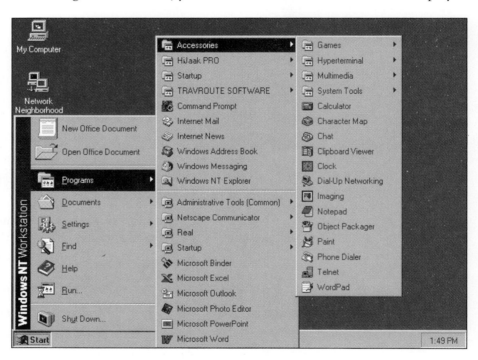

FIGURE 1-13
A series of menus

4. Position the pointer anywhere over the Desktop away from the menus.

5. Click the left mouse button.

All menus are removed from the Desktop.

USING THE RIGHT MOUSE BUTTON

shortcut menu A list of an item's most frequently used commands.

In Windows NT, right mouse button use has been standardized. Clicking an item with the right button displays its **shortcut menu**, a list of the item's most frequently used commands.

OPENING A SHORTCUT MENU FOR A SYSTEM ICON

In the following steps, you will use the right mouse button to display the shortcut menu for a system icon.

HANDS ON

1. Point to the My Computer system icon.

2. Click the right mouse button.

My Computer's shortcut menu appears, as shown in Figure 1-14.

FIGURE 1-14

My Computer's shortcut menu

3. Select Open.

The My Computer window appears.

OPENING A SHORTCUT MENU FOR A DEVICE ICON

device A piece of equipment (hardware), such as a printer or disk drive, that is part of your computer system.

A **device** is a piece of equipment, such as a printer or disk drive, that is part of your computer system. **Device icons** allow you to customize and use these pieces of equipment. In the following steps, you will use the right mouse button to display the shortcut menu for a device icon and select a device icon command.

HANDS ON

1. Make sure the My Computer window is open on the Desktop.

2. Point to the drive C: icon in the My Computer window.

Drive C: is usually a hard disk drive. It may be built into your computer or connected to it by a cable.

device icon A small image that represents a hardware device, such as a printer or disk drive, installed on the computer system.

3. Click the right mouse button.

The device icon shortcut menu appears.

4. Select Properties.

The Properties dialog box for disk drive C: appears, as shown in Figure 1-15. This dialog box provides detailed information about the C: drive.

5. Click the Close button for the Properties dialog box.

6. Click the Close button for the My Computer window.

The My Computer window is removed from the Desktop.

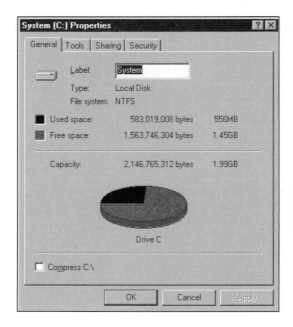

FIGURE 1-15

*The Drive C: Properties
dialog box*

OPENING AND CANCELING TASKBAR SHORTCUT MENUS

In the following steps, you will practice using the right mouse button to open specific taskbar shortcut menus; then you will practice canceling these menus with the mouse.

HANDS ON

1. Point to the taskbar's Start button.

2. Click the right mouse button.

   The Start button's shortcut menu appears.

3. Position the pointer anywhere over the Desktop, away from the taskbar.

4. Click the left mouse button.

   The Start button's shortcut menu is removed from the Desktop.

5. Point to the Clock on the right end of the taskbar.

   Today's date briefly appears and vanishes.

6. Click the right mouse button.

   The Clock's shortcut menu appears, with different commands from the Start shortcut menu.

7. Position the pointer anywhere over an empty area on the Desktop.

8. Click the left mouse button.

   The menu is removed from the Desktop.

WORKING WITH A GRAPHICAL USER INTERFACE

You have already seen many features of a graphical user interface (GUI). You have used the mouse to choose commands, start programs, and view windows by pointing and clicking. As its name implies, GUIs are extremely visual.

Icons represent devices, software, shortcuts, and other objects. Windows display icon contents. You use the mouse to tell the software what you want to do, such as access menus, run application software, and position objects on the screen.

WYSIWYG An acronym for *What You See Is What You Get,* a GUI characteristic in which documents appear on screen much as they will appear on a printed page.

All Windows programs are graphical. They share so many common elements that you may forget which program you are using. With a Windows program, the graphical environment is described as "what you see is what you get" (abbreviated as **WYSIWYG**). This means that text and graphics print exactly as they appear on screen.

DIALOG BOXES

dialog box A rectangle containing a set of options that appears when Windows NT needs more information from the user in order to perform a requested operation.

When you choose certain commands or menu options, a window appears in the middle of the screen. This window is called a **dialog box** because it requests more information concerning your selection. Menu options that display dialog boxes are followed by ellipses (...) such as Shut Down in Figure 1-16. Figure 1-17 shows the Shut Down Windows dialog box.

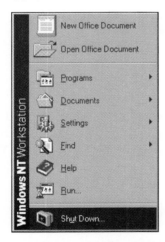

FIGURE 1-16
The Start menu with ellipsis menu item

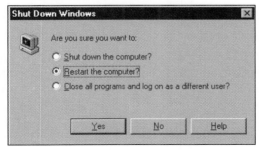

FIGURE 1-17
The Shut Down Windows dialog box

TEXT BOXES

text box A rectangular control that displays the name or value of a current setting and in which you can type a different name or value to change the setting.

Next to some options you will see rectangular boxes into which you can type, as shown in Figure 1-18. These are called **text boxes**. Sometimes text boxes already have characters in them. In these cases, the letters or numbers in the box are the default value. A **default** is a value that the software uses unless you tell it otherwise. When the characters in the box are highlighted, any characters you type replace the highlighted text.

FIGURE 1-18

A text box

COMMAND BUTTONS

default A value or setting that software uses automatically unless you specify a different value or setting.

Clickable command buttons are common dialog box features. A single click on these buttons performs the action listed on the button. Nearly every dialog box has the three essential buttons shown in Figure 1-19:

- *OK* (Uses your settings and closes the dialog box.)

- *Apply* (Uses your settings but keeps the dialog box open to make other selections.)

- *Cancel* (Closes the dialog box without making any changes.)

FIGURE 1-19

Three essential command buttons

RADIO BUTTONS

radio button A small circle which is filled with a solid dot when the button is selected; only one in a set of radio buttons can be selected.

Some dialog boxes contain a group of round buttons, as shown in Figure 1-20. These are called **radio buttons**. Only one button in a set of radio buttons can be selected; that button has a solid dot. When you click on an empty radio button, it becomes selected and the previous selection is deselected.

FIGURE 1-20

Radio buttons

TRIANGLE BUTTONS AND DROP-DOWN LISTS

triangle button A button in the shape of a small downward-pointing triangle, which displays a menu of options when clicked.

drop-down list A list of options displayed when you click a triangle button.

Some text boxes allow you to pick from a predetermined list of options. These boxes have a **triangle button** to their right, as shown in Figure 1-21. Clicking this triangle button displays a **drop-down list** of options, as shown in Figure 1-22. The list remains on the screen until you click an option to choose it or click outside the list to cancel the display.

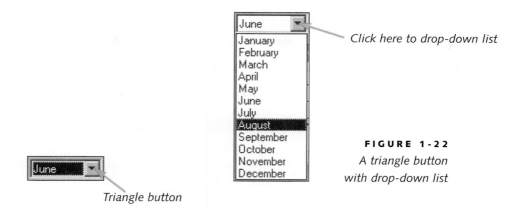

Click here to drop-down list

FIGURE 1-22

*A triangle button
with drop-down list*

FIGURE 1-21

A triangle button

Triangle button

COUNTER BUTTONS

counter button A control used to change a numerical setting, consisting of an up arrow above a down arrow; clicking the up arrow increases the setting; clicking the down arrow decreases it.

A text box that contains numbers will often have a counter button to its right, as shown in Figure 1-23. A **counter button** is an up arrow above a down arrow, each in its own box. Clicking the up arrow increases the number; clicking the down arrow decreases the number.

FIGURE 1-23

A counter button

Counter button

CHECK BOXES

check box A square in a dialog box that contains a ✓ when an option is selected or appears empty when the option is not selected.

A square box to the left of a dialog box option, as shown in Figure 1-24, is known as a **check box**. Clicking an empty check box puts a check mark in the box to select that item. Clicking on a check box with a check mark already in it deselects the item and erases the ✓. Unlike radio buttons, you can select more than one check box.

FIGURE 1-24

A check box

☑ Automatically adjust clock for daylight saving changes

Check box

USING DIALOG BOX OPTIONS

control panel A dialog box that lets you change settings on your computer.

Control panels are dialog boxes that let you change the settings on your computer. Here you will open control panel dialog boxes and use various buttons to change the settings on your computer.

WARNING

Do not make any changes other than those described here, or you may inappropriately change the settings on the computer you are using.

HANDS ON

1. Double-click the My Computer icon.

The My Computer window appears on the Desktop.

2. Double-click the Control Panel folder.

The Control Panel window appears.

3. Double-click the Date/Time control panel icon.

The Date/Time Properties dialog box appears, as shown in Figure 1-25.

Use these buttons to change the year

Click here to select a different month

To change the time, select the value in this box and type the correct time, or use the buttons

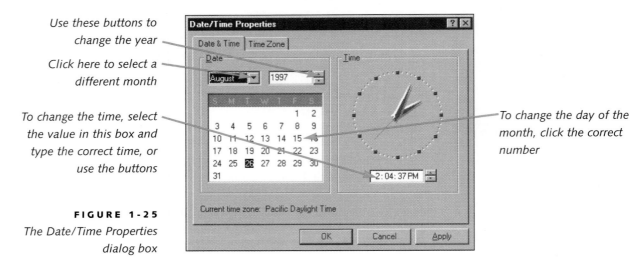

To change the day of the month, click the correct number

FIGURE 1-25
The Date/Time Properties dialog box

4. Click the Month triangle button in the set of Date options.

A list of months drops down.

5. Select October.

6. Click 30 in the box of days for the selected month.

The Current Day setting highlights.

7. Double-click on the Current Hour number in the set of Time options.

8. Type 11 (or click the counter buttons as many times as is necessary to change the setting to 11).

T I P

You can increment the number faster by pressing and holding the left mouse button while the pointer is over a counter button. You can also do this by pressing and holding ↑ or ↓ on the keyboard.

9. Select the Current Minutes number, and use either the mouse or keyboard to change the setting to 59.

10. Select the Current Seconds number, and use either the mouse or keyboard to change the setting to 45.

11. If necessary, change the AM/PM indicator to PM.

12. Select Apply.

The new settings are applied to the system's internal clock. Watch the clock in the dialog box after you've applied the changes. It switches to the selected time, and the second hand begins moving. After the time changes to 12:00 AM, notice that the day setting changes to 31.

RESETTING THE SYSTEM'S INTERNAL CLOCK

In the following steps, you will reset the current date and time settings to reflect today's date and the current time.

HANDS ON

1. Make sure the Date/Time Properties dialog box is open on the Desktop.

NOTE   *Repeat steps 1 through 3 in the previous activity, if necessary, to open the Date/Time Properties dialog box.*

2. Select the appropriate month, day, hour, and minutes settings to reflect today's date and the current time.

3. Change the AM/PM indicator, if necessary.

4. Select Apply.

   The changes are applied to the system's internal clock.

5. Select OK.

   The changes are stored and the dialog box is removed from the Desktop.

6. Click the Close buttons for the Control Panel and My Computer windows, respectively.

   Both windows are removed from the Desktop.

LOGGING OFF WINDOWS NT 4.0

log off Inform the operating system that the current user is no longer working on the computer.

Just as organized people clear their desks before leaving the office for the day, you should develop the habit of closing all open applications and using the proper procedure to **log off** Windows NT when you are finished working with the computer. In fact, turning off the computer while applications are running is dangerous. Some of the work you have been doing may not have been saved onto disk and will be irretrievably lost. In addition, you will not have given the operating system the opportunity to erase information it may have temporarily stored on disk. Logging off also prevents unauthorized access to the computer. Before the computer can be used again, a valid user name and password must be entered.

Follow these steps to log off the Windows NT operating system. You will be able to start and quit Windows at any point in the lessons that follow.

HANDS ON

1. Click the taskbar's Start button.

   The Start menu appears.

2. Select Shut Down.

   The entire screen darkens a bit, and the Shut Down Windows dialog box appears, as shown in Figure 1-26. Notice that the Close All Programs And Log On As A Different User? option is selected automatically.

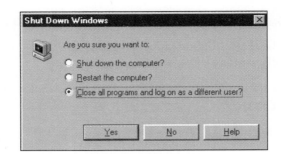

FIGURE 1-26
*The Shut Down Windows
dialog box*

3. Select Yes.

After a few moments, the Windows NT logo screen appears with the Begin Logon window over it.

N O T E   *If necessary, and you have permission, you may turn off the computer by selecting the Shut Down Computer option. When the screen tells you, turn off the computer's power switch. If your monitor has a separate power switch, turn this off as well.*

LESSON SUMMARY AND EXERCISES

After you complete this lesson, you should know how to do the following:

INTRODUCING OPERATING SYSTEM SOFTWARE

- Understand the components of a computer system and the function of the operating system.

STARTING THE COMPUTER WITH WINDOWS NT 4.0

- Turn on the computer and load the Windows NT 4.0 operating system.

USING THE WINDOWS NT DESKTOP

- Identify the main components of the Windows NT screen, including the taskbar and Desktop icons.

USING THE MOUSE

- Use the mouse to point to objects and menu items on the screen.
- Click the left mouse button to select objects or menu items on the screen.
- Double-click the left mouse button to perform an action on a selected icon or screen object.
- Drag-and-drop objects on the Desktop. Click and hold the left mouse button while pointing to an object. Move the mouse to move the object on the screen. Release the mouse button when the object is in the desired location.

USING THE RIGHT MOUSE BUTTON

- Click the right mouse button to display the shortcut menu appropriate to the action you are performing.

WORKING WITH A GRAPHICAL USER INTERFACE

- Type information into a text box within a dialog box. Highlighted text in the text box is the default value. Typing new text replaces the highlighted text in the box.
- Click command buttons in a dialog box. Click OK after you have concluded your selections. Click Cancel to quit the dialog box without making any changes.
- Click radio buttons to make a choice between several possible actions. Only one button can be in effect at a time.
- Select choices from drop-down lists by holding down the button to see the choices.
- Increase or decrease numbers in a box by using counter buttons.
- Make selections by using check boxes. Check boxes have a check mark in them when the option is selected and are empty when not selected.

LOGGING OFF WINDOWS NT 4.0

- Log off the computer by using the Shut Down option that appears as a choice in the Start menu. Using the Shut Down option ensures that data is saved and temporary files are erased before you log off the computer.

NEW TERMS TO REMEMBER

After you complete this lesson, you should know the meaning of these terms:

application	log on
booting the system	menu
button	mouse pointer
check box	open
clicking	operating system (software)
close	password
commands	pointer
control panel	pointing
counter button	Power On Self Test (POST)
default	radio button
deselect	select
Desktop	shortcut icon
device	shortcut menu
device icon	software
dialog box	system boot
double-click	system icon
dragging	taskbar
drag-and-drop	text box
drop-down list	triangle button
graphical user interface (GUI)	user interface
hardware	user name
highlight	window
icon	WYSIWYG
log off	

MATCHING EXERCISE

Match each of the terms with the definitions on the right:

TERMS	DEFINITIONS
1. clicking	**a.** On-screen arrow pointing to the upper-left corner of the screen that can be moved with the mouse
2. dialog box	**b.** Mouse action or technique used to position the pointer in a specific location
3. drag-and-drop	**c.** Rectangular object that displays an application program, a document, and other features and that can be sized and positioned anywhere on screen
4. graphical user interface	**d.** Element at the very bottom of the screen that contains the Start button, the Clock indicator, and buttons for any open application
5. icons	**e.** Mouse action or technique in which an object is moved from one location to another
6. mouse pointer	**f.** Operating system in which commands and options are represented by pictures or icons that can be selected with a mouse
7. pointing	**g.** Characteristic of a graphical user interface (GUI) in which the appearance of a document or image on screen very closely resembles its appearance when printed on paper
8. taskbar	**h.** Rectangular object that displays one or more options a user can select to provide a program with the additional information necessary to carry out a command
9. window	**i.** Mouse action or technique in which a button is pressed (and released) once very quickly
10. WYSIWYG	**j.** Graphic pictures or on-screen objects that represent commands or programs, which carry out an operation when selected with the mouse

COMPLETION EXERCISE

Fill in the missing word or phrase for each of the following:

1. _____ in dialog boxes contain a check mark when the option is chosen.

2. _____ is a technique in which a mouse button is pressed and released twice very rapidly, such as to open a window.

3. In some dialog boxes you can type information in a(n) _____ to supply a program with the additional information necessary to complete a command operation.

4. In some dialog boxes you can select from a set of options that appear on a(n) _____.

5. For some elements on screen in the Windows NT environment, you can click the _____ mouse button to display a shortcut menu.

6. The _____ consists of the hardware, applications software, and the user.

7. To help you remember and choose them, lists of commands and options appear on _____.

8. _____ appear as small images on the Desktop or in windows and dialog boxes.

9. A(n) _____ setting is one that the computer, or an applications program, uses automatically until the user specifies another.

10. _____ is an acronym for "what you see is what you get."

SHORT-ANSWER QUESTIONS

Write a brief answer to each of the following questions:

1. Describe an example of a user's direct interaction with an operating system and an example of a user's indirect interaction with an operating system.

2. Briefly describe what occurs during a computer's Power-On Self Test (POST).

3. List three ways in which you can use the taskbar.

4. What is selection? How do you do it and why is it important to Windows NT?

5. List and briefly describe the different types of options that can be available in dialog boxes.

6. What is a device? What are some of the device icons that you might see on your computer screen?

7. As you explore Windows NT, you might open dialog boxes with settings you do not understand. OK, Apply, and Cancel are three buttons you will see on most dialog boxes. What is the function of each? Which button is safest to click with an unfamiliar dialog box, and why?

8. In this lesson you learned the basic mouse actions. What is the difference between pointing, clicking, double-clicking, and dragging (and dropping)?

9. What is meant by a user interface? A graphical user interface?

10. What steps should you follow to end a computing session?

APPLICATION PROJECTS

Perform the following actions to complete these projects:

1. Practice some mouse techniques by doing the following.

Select (highlight) the My Computer icon. Position the pointer over the selected icon and click the right mouse button. Then select Open. Click the My Computer window's Close button. Drag the My Computer icon to the lower-left corner of the Desktop. Double-click the My Computer icon and then double-click the Control Panel icon. Then click both windows' Close buttons. Drag the My Computer icon back to its original location.

2. Position the pointer over the taskbar's Clock, click the right mouse button, and then select Properties. Select the Date/Time Properties dialog box's Time Zone tab, if necessary. Display the drop-down list of time zone options, and select the option (GMT-10:00) Hawaii. Select the Date/Time tab and note the change to the time setting. Click the Date/Time Properties dialog box's Cancel button.

3. Windows NT often provides more than one way to accomplish the same task. Follow these steps to practice three different ways to open the Control Panel folder icon. Determine which method you prefer and state why. Begin by double-clicking My Computer to display the Control Panel folder icon.

First way:

  a. Point to the Control Panel icon.

  b. Click with the right mouse button to display the icon's shortcut menu.

  c. Choose Open.

  d. Once the Control Panel window opens, click its Close button to close its window.

Second way:

  a. Point to the Control Panel icon.

  b. Choose Open from the File menu.

  c. Once the Control Panel window opens, click its Close button to close its window.

Third way:

  a. Double-click the Control Panel folder icon.

  b. Once the Control Panel window opens, click its Close button to close its window.

4. Beginning at the Desktop with all windows closed and menus hidden, make your own step-by-step instructions to do each of the following:

    a. Open the C: drive window.

    b. Display the Date/Time shortcuts menu.

    c. Identify Start menu items that lead to a dialog box.

5. Many dialog boxes have the same three buttons: OK, Apply, and Cancel. Follow these steps to observe the difference between these three commands:

Change Date and Apply:

    a. Open the Date/Time Properties dialog box.

    b. Set the date for January 1, 2055.

    c. Click the Apply button. Does the dialog box close?

    d. Point to the Clock button on the taskbar. What date is displayed?

Change Date and Cancel:

    a. Check that the Date/Time Properties dialog box is still open.

    b. Set the date for October 31, 1999.

    c. Click the Cancel button. Does the dialog box close?

    d. Point to the Clock button on the taskbar. What date is displayed?

Change Date and OK:

    a. Check that the Date/Time Properties dialog box is still open.

    b. Set the date for today's current date.

    c. Click the OK button. Does the dialog box close?

    d. Point to the Clock button on the taskbar. What date is displayed?

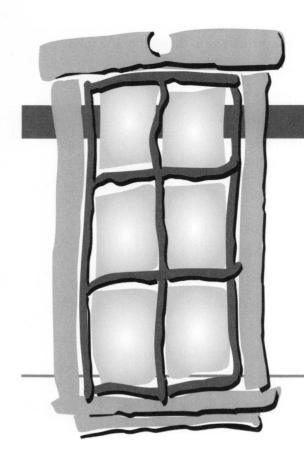

LESSON 2

WORKING WITH WINDOWS

OBJECTIVES

After you complete this lesson, you will be able to do the following:

- *Recognize the common window elements, such as the title bar, menu bar, and scroll bars.*

- *Size, minimize, maximize, and restore windows.*

- *Display multiple windows on the Desktop simultaneously.*

- *Find Help on Windows NT topics.*

A dictionary might define the word "window" as "an opening, set in a frame, for looking outside of a structure or letting in light and air." While you usually think of windows in a house or a car, computer windows are frames on the screen, through which you view documents, programs, and information. Unlike the windows in your home, you can close windows on the computer so that they are completely invisible. The size and position of windows are determined by you, the user.

In this lesson, you will learn all about windows—how to open, close, size, and position them, and how to move through the information contained in them. When you have mastered the techniques for working with windows, you will be well on your way to mastering Windows NT.

WORKING WITH WINDOWS

maximize A Windows sizing feature in which an open window is enlarged to fill the screen; also, the name of the button which performs this function.

minimize A Windows sizing feature which reduces an open window to a button on the taskbar; also, the name of the button which performs this function.

size To change the dimensions of a window so that its contents remain visible, but the window occupies only a portion of the Desktop.

All the work you do in Windows NT takes place inside of windows. Most Windows NT objects are in icon form, represented by their small on-screen picture. To work on a specific letter, a budget, an application, a control panel, or other Windows NT object, you must open its icon to see its window. Then, as you use the object, you change appearance, size, and location of its window for efficient work.

To give an object as much workspace as possible, you **maximize** or expand its window to fill the entire screen. To keep an object available but hidden, you **minimize** its window to a taskbar button. To confine an object to only a portion of the Desktop, you **size** or change the dimensions of that window. You can see the contents of the sized window, but the window takes up less than the full screen.

Windows can overlap each other, partially hiding windows behind them. You can move windows around on the Desktop and even change the size of the window. In the exercises that follow you will develop the skills required to manipulate windows—they are, after all, the elements that give the Windows NT operating system its name.

COMPONENTS AND TYPES OF WINDOWS

Figure 2-1 shows you the major components of each window.

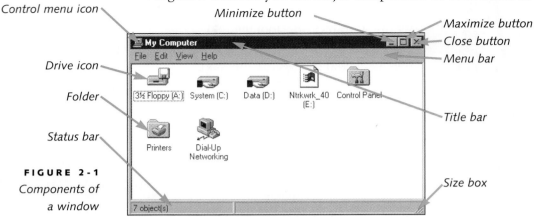

Control menu icon

Minimize button

Maximize button

Close button

Drive icon

Menu bar

Folder

Status bar

Title bar

FIGURE 2-1
*Components of
a window*

Size box

THE TITLE BAR

title bar An area at the top of a window that displays the name of the application, document, or device which the window represents.

active window The window ready to accept input from the mouse or keyboard, indicated by a colored title bar; only one open window is active.

inactive window Any window that will not accept mouse or keyboard input until it is made active; inactive windows have clear or gray title bars.

Across the top of the window is the **title bar**. The name of the object appears in the title bar. When the title bar has a color such as blue or pink, its window is **active**—ready to accept your input from the mouse or keyboard. Only one window can be active at any given time. Any other windows on the Desktop will have clear or gray title bars, indicating that they are **inactive**—temporarily out of use.

On the left side of the title bar is the **control menu icon**. Clicking this button displays a menu that, among other options, lets you minimize, maximize, or close its window. On the right side of the title bar are buttons that maximize, minimize, or close the window with a single click of the left mouse button. A maximized window has a **Restore** rather than a Maximize button. The Restore button shrinks the maximized window to its previous size and location.

THE MENU BAR

control menu icon In Windows, a small control, typically on the left side of the title bar, that when clicked displays a menu for manipulating the window.

Below the title bar is the **menu bar**. It contains the names of menus you can use within this window. Although menu names vary, the leftmost menu name is almost always File and the rightmost, Help. Clicking a menu name displays its menu options below its name, such as the File menu in Figure 2-2.

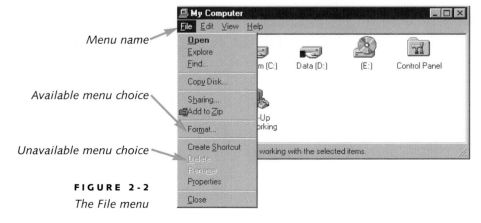

Menu name

Available menu choice

Unavailable menu choice

FIGURE 2-2
The File menu

restore (1) To return a maximized window to its previous size; also the name of the button that performs this function; (2) To return a deleted item to its original location, generally from the Recyle Bin.

menu bar An area below the title bar of all application windows containing the names of menus which, when clicked, displays a list of commands.

Menu options are context-sensitive, and not all may be available at any given time. Available menu items are dark, such as Open or Close in Figure 2-2; unavailable menu options are dimmed, such as Delete or Rename in the same figure.

Once the menu is displayed, its first option is highlighted. Moving the mouse toward you moves the highlight down the list. When the highlight covers the option you want, you can choose it by clicking the left button. To leave a menu without choosing an option, either click the menu name or move outside the menu and click.

You can also use the keyboard to make menu selections.

■ To select a menu name, hold down Alt on the keyboard and press the letter underlined in the name, such as Alt + F to display the File menu.

■ To select a menu option, use ↑ or ↓ to highlight the desired option and then press Enter. Alternatively, you can type the underlined letter of the desired option, such as O for Open.

■ To close a menu without choosing an option, press Esc. Press Esc a second time to remove the highlight from the menu name.

Some options have keyboard shortcut keys printed beside them. The shortcut keys displayed on the menu serve as a reminder that you can select the option without going to the menu. For example, you might see F3 beside the Save As option on some File menus. This means that a third way exists to select the option. You can click the File menu and click Save As; hold down Alt, type **f**, and select Save As; or just press F3.

POSITIONING AND SIZING WINDOWS

You can place windows on the screen and change their sizes using the mouse.

POSITIONING WINDOWS

To move a window to a new location, point to the title bar, click and hold the left button of the mouse, move the mouse to drag the window, and release the button when the window is at the desired location.

NOTE   *On some screens, you may only see the outline of the window move. When you release the button, the contents of the window will appear in place of the outline.*

MOVING A WINDOW

In the following steps, you will practice moving a window.

HANDS ON

1. If necessary, log on to Windows NT.

2. Double-click the My Computer icon.

The My Computer window opens.

3. Point to the title bar.

4. Press and hold the left mouse button, and then drag the My Computer window down to the lower-right corner of the screen, as shown in Figure 2-3. Release the mouse button to set the position of the My Computer window.

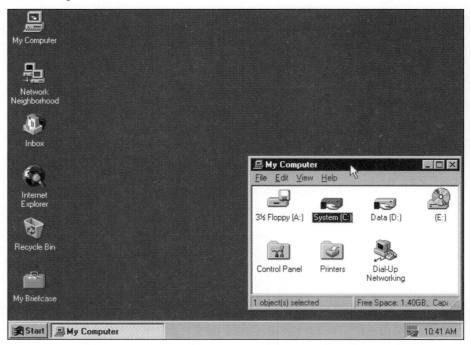

FIGURE 2-3

A moved window

SIZING WINDOWS

When you move the pointer to the edge of a window, the pointer changes shape to indicate the direction in which the window edge can move. A pointer on the left or right edge of a window becomes a horizontal double-headed arrow; moving the pointer to the top or bottom edge of the window changes the pointer to a vertical double-headed arrow. By moving the pointer to one of these locations, you can drag that window edge to change the size of the window. For example, dragging the left edge of the window to the right makes a narrower window; dragging the bottom edge down makes a longer window.

If you move the pointer to one of the four corners of the window, the pointer becomes a diagonal double-headed arrow. Dragging a corner of the window stretches or shrinks two sides simultaneously. You can move a window by clicking the control menu icon and selecting the Move command. A four-way arrow appears and you can then move the window. Figure 2-4 shows the various pointers you can use to size and move windows.

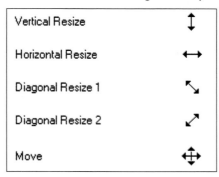

FIGURE 2-4

Pointers for sizing and moving windows

OPENING A WINDOW FROM THE KEYBOARD

In the following steps, you will use the keyboard to open another window.

HANDS ON

1. Click the Control Panel folder to select it.

The Control Panel folder icon highlights to show it is selected.

2. Hold down the [Alt] key and press and release the [F] key. Release the [Alt] key.

The File menu appears, as shown in Figure 2-2.

3. Press and release the [O] key.

The Control Panel window opens on top of the My Computer window. Notice that each window contains its own title and menu bars.

CHANGING THE SIZE OF A WINDOW

In the following steps, you will use standard Windows features to change the sizes of open windows.

HANDS ON

1. Click the Maximize button on the Control Panel window.

The selected window enlarges to cover the full screen.

2. Click the Minimize button.

The Control Panel window closes, replaced by its taskbar button, as shown in Figure 2-5.

FIGURE 2-5

The Control Panel's taskbar button

Control Panel

3. Point to the right edge of the My Computer window.

The pointer changes to a horizontal, double-headed arrow.

4. Press and hold the left mouse button, and then drag the window so that it is approximately the size shown in Figure 2-6. Release the mouse button to reduce the size of the window.

5. Click the Maximize button on the My Computer window.

The window enlarges to cover the full screen. Notice that the Maximize button has been replaced by a Restore button.

6. Click the Restore button on the My Computer window.

The window reduces to the size it was before it was maximized to full-screen size.

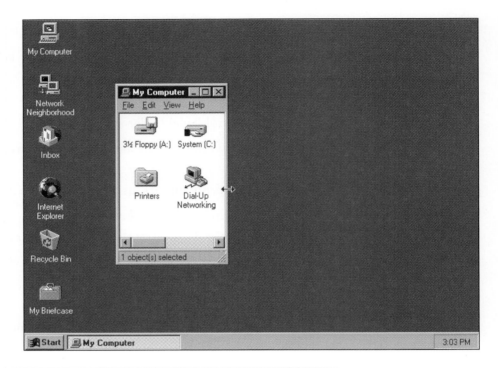

FIGURE 2-6

*Resizing the
My Computer window*

CHANGING THE SIZE OF ANOTHER WINDOW

In the following steps, you will drag selected borders to change the size of the My Computer window.

**HANDS
ON**

1. Point to the top border of the My Computer window.

   Notice that the pointer changes to a vertical, double-headed arrow.

2. Drag the top border outline up to near the top of the screen and release the mouse.

   The window expands vertically.

3. Point to the right border of the window.

   Notice that the pointer changes to a horizontal, double-headed arrow.

4. Drag the right border near to the right edge of the screen.

   The window expands horizontally to resemble Figure 2-7.

ARRANGING MULTIPLE WINDOWS WITH THE TASKBAR MENU

Occasions may occur when several application windows are open. Although you can position and size individual windows using the techniques you have just learned, it is faster to use the arrangement commands built into Windows NT: cascade, tile horizontal, and tile vertical.

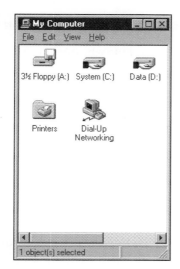

FIGURE 2-7

The My Computer window with new dimensions

CASCADING WINDOWS

cascade A technique for arranging open windows in equal size and stacked, so that only the top window is fully visible and the upper-left corners of the other windows appear behind it.

Cascading open windows sizes them proportionately and stacks them, one upon another, so that only the top window is fully visible, as shown in Figure 2-8. When you cascade windows, the window that is active when you select the Cascade command appears on top of the stack, but all of the windows are inactive. To activate a window, you click on any visible portion of that window (for example, its title bar). Activating a partially hidden window brings it to the top of the stack.

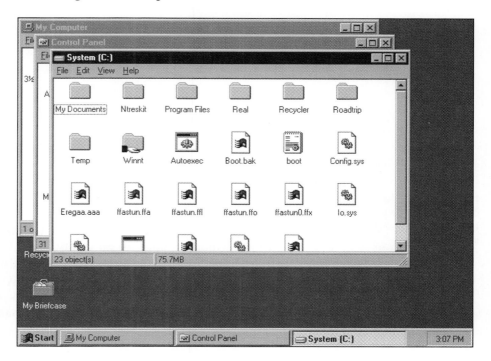

FIGURE 2-8

Three open windows in a cascade arrangement

OPENING AND CASCADING MULTIPLE WINDOWS

In the following steps, you will open and display windows in a cascade arrangement.

HANDS ON

1. Make sure the My Computer window is open on the Desktop and that the Control Panel button appears on the taskbar.

NOTE   *If the Control Panel button does not appear on the taskbar, double-click its icon in the My Computer window, select the Control Panel window's Maximize button, and then select its Minimize button.*

2. Double-click the C: drive icon to open it.

Its window will appear on the Desktop. Your window objects will probably be different than the ones in Figure 2-8.

3. Click the Control Panel button on the taskbar.

The Control Panel window opens on the Desktop in full-screen size, hiding the other two windows.

4. Point to an empty area on the taskbar.

5. Click the right mouse button.

The shortcut menu for the taskbar appears, as shown in Figure 2-9.

FIGURE 2-9

The taskbar shortcut menu

6. Click Cascade Windows.

The open windows are sized equally and cascade on the Desktop (similar to those shown in Figure 2-8).

TILING WINDOWS

tile A technique for arranging open windows side by side and equally sized so that all are fully visible.

Tiling open windows sizes them equally and arranges them, either horizontally or vertically, so that they occupy equal portions of the Desktop. Figure 2-10 shows open windows tiled in a horizontal arrangement.

To tile windows, point to an empty part of the taskbar, and then click the right button to display the taskbar shortcut menu shown in Figure 2-9. Then select Tile Windows Horizontally or Tile Windows Vertically. To select (activate) another tiled window, you would click anywhere on that window. When you tile windows, the active window remains active.

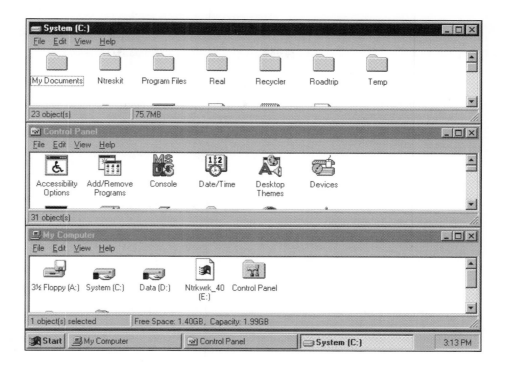

FIGURE 2-10

Three open windows tiled horizontally

TILING MULTIPLE WINDOWS HORIZONTALLY

In the following steps, you will tile the open windows horizontally on the Desktop.

HANDS ON

1. Point to an empty area on the taskbar.

2. Click the right mouse button.

The taskbar shortcut menu appears.

3. Click Tile Windows Horizontally.

The three open windows are sized equally and arranged horizontally so they each occupy approximately one-third of the Desktop area, as shown in Figure 2-10.

TILING MULTIPLE WINDOWS VERTICALLY

In the following steps, you will tile the open windows vertically on the Desktop.

HANDS ON

1. Point to an empty area on the taskbar.

2. Click the right mouse button.

The taskbar shortcut menu appears.

3. Click Tile Windows Vertically.

The open windows are sized equally and arranged vertically so they each occupy approximately one-third of the Desktop area (similar to those shown in Figure 2-11).

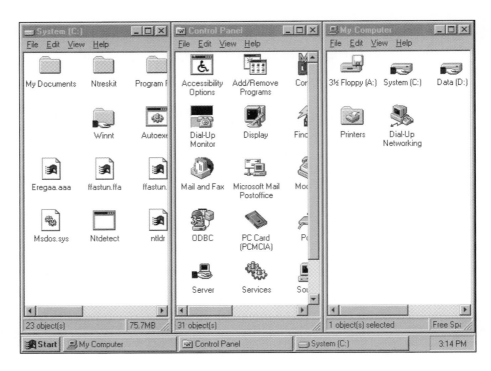

FIGURE 2-11
*Three open windows
tiled vertically*

After you have arranged application windows with either the Cascade command or one of the Tile commands, you can still size or position any window. Keep in mind that if you maximize any window to full size and then later select its Restore button, the open windows will return to the same arrangement that existed before you enlarged the window. For example, if you maximize the Control Panel window among windows in a cascade arrangement and then later select its Restore button, the open windows will again cascade on the Desktop with the Control Panel window on top of the stack.

MINIMIZING ALL OPEN WINDOWS

Sometimes you want to minimize all Desktop windows to give yourself a clean workspace. In the following steps, you will minimize all open windows in a single operation.

**HANDS
ON**

1. Point to an empty area on the taskbar.

2. Click the right mouse button.

The shortcut menu for the taskbar appears.

3. Click Minimize All Windows.

All open windows are minimized, and their corresponding buttons appear on the taskbar.

ARRANGING ICONS

You can also move and position icons on the Desktop. To position an icon, drag it to the desired location and drop it. (Be careful not to click or double-click the icon unless you intend to work with the program.) Program icons tend to stay where you put them. If you have a lot of icons on the Desktop, they might be scattered around—they might become hidden behind other icons or windows. To display the icons in neat rows, use the Arrange Icons command on the shortcut menu that appears when you click the right mouse button with the pointer over any empty area on the Desktop.

ARRANGING DESKTOP ICONS

In the following steps, you will practice arranging the Desktop icons.

HANDS ON

1. Make sure all open windows are minimized.

2. Drag the My Computer system icon to the bottom right corner of the Desktop.

NOTE   *If the My Computer icon won't hold its position, the Auto Arrange command on the Desktop is on. To turn it off, position the pointer over an empty part of the Desktop, click the right mouse button, highlight the Arrange Icons command, and then select Auto Arrange. Now retry step 2.*

3. Drag the Recycle Bin system icon to the center of the Desktop.

4. Move any other icons on your Desktop to other places on the screen.

5. Point to an empty area of the Desktop.

6. Click the right mouse button.

The Desktop shortcut menu appears.

7. Highlight Arrange Icons, and then click Auto Arrange from the next pop-up menu.

toggle   A command or an option that can be turned on and off by repeatedly clicking the command or option.

The Desktop's system icons align vertically along the left edge of the Desktop (screen).

NOTE   *Auto Arrange is a **toggle** command: the first time you choose it, it turns on; the next time you choose it, it turns off. When it is on, a check mark appears before its name on the Desktop shortcut menu.*

ARRANGING WINDOW ICONS

In the following steps, you will practice arranging icons within an open window.

HANDS ON

1. Make sure all open windows are minimized.

2. In the taskbar, click the Control Panel button.

The Control Panel window opens on the Desktop in the size it last appeared before it was minimized.

3. Click the View menu.

The View menu appears.

4. Highlight Arrange Icons.

Another menu appears. Your menus will resemble Figure 2-12.

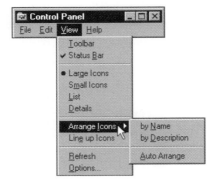

FIGURE 2-12

Locating the Arrange Icons menu option

5. Click Auto Arrange.

The icons for the Control Panel window rearrange themselves, as shown in Figure 2-13.

FIGURE 2-13

The Control Panel window's rearranged icons

6. Point to the upper-left corner of the Control Panel window.

The pointer changes to a diagonal, double-headed arrow.

7. Drag this corner of the window down and to the left and release, to size the window as shown in Figure 2-14.

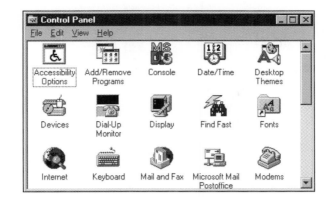

FIGURE 2-14

*The sized
Control Panel window*

Notice that because you have toggled on the Auto Arrange feature, the icons rearrange themselves whenever you resize the window.

CHANGING THE SIZE OF A WINDOW'S ICONS

large icon An icon displayed at full-size.

small icon An icon displayed at quarter size.

Windows NT allows you to view icons in two different sizes. **Large icons** are easy to distinguish, but they take up more room. **Small icons** are about a quarter of the size of large ones, so many more can be seen in a window. In the following steps, you will modify the size of icons displayed in an open window.

HANDS ON

1. In the Control Panel, click the View menu.

The View menu appears.

2. Click Small Icons.

The icons change to a smaller display size.

3. Click the View menu.

4. Point to Arrange Icons, and then click By Name on the pop-up menu.

The icons rearrange to conform to the shape of the window. Notice that they are also arranged alphabetically by name.

5. Click the View menu.

6. Click Large Icons.

The icons appear in a larger display size.

USING SCROLL BARS

scroll bar A rectangular bar that appears along the right or bottom of a window when not all the window's contents are visible and which is used to bring the contents into view.

A **scroll bar** appears along the right or bottom side of a window when there is not enough room to display all of the contents of the window. If the unseen information is above or below that viewed in the window, you see a **vertical scroll bar**; if the information is to the left or right, you see a **horizontal scroll bar**. Both scroll bars are illustrated in Figure 2-15.

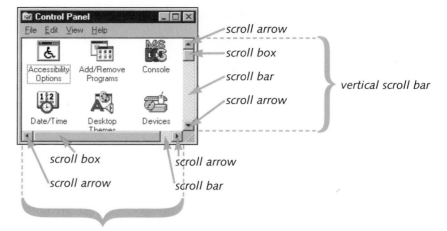

FIGURE 2-15

An open window's scroll bars, arrows, and boxes

vertical scroll bar A rectangular bar that appears along the right side of a window that is too short to display all its contents; clicking or dragging in the scroll bar brings additional contents into view.

horizontal scroll bar A rectangular bar that appears along the bottom of a window that is too narrow to display all its contents; clicking or dragging in the scroll bar brings additional contents into view.

Within the scroll bar is a rectangle known as the **scroll box**. This box indicates the relative position of the screen information within its window. If the scroll box is at the top or left of the scroll bar, you are viewing the top or left part of the information. If the scroll box is at the bottom or right of the scroll bar, you are viewing the bottom or right of the information. Clicking the scroll bar shifts the display to view another screen of information. Clicking below the scroll box on a vertical scroll bar displays the next screen of information. Clicking above the scroll box displays the previous screen. You can also drag-and-drop the scroll box to move quickly to the desired position within a document or list of information.

Scroll arrows at either end of the scroll bar allow slow window navigation. Clicking a scroll arrow moves one line up or down on a vertical list, or right or left on a horizontal scroll bar. Pressing a scroll arrow permits line by line scrolling in the direction the arrow points.

SCROLLING A WINDOW'S CONTENTS VERTICALLY

In the following steps, you will practice using scroll bars to scroll the contents of a window.

HANDS ON

scroll box A rectangle in a scroll bar that can be dragged to display information; its location represents the location of the visible information in relation to the window's entire contents.

scroll arrows Buttons in a scroll bar that let you scroll information in a window in small increments—for example, scrolling text line by line.

1. Display the Control Panel window if it is not already visible, and size it so that it looks similar to Figure 2-15.

2. Click Auto Arrange from the Arrange Icons submenu of the View menu to toggle this option off.

3. Point to the vertical scroll bar, anywhere below its scroll box and click.

The column of icons appears to scroll upward as the scroll box moves downward.

4. If the scroll box is not already at the bottom of the vertical scroll bar, point to the vertical scroll bar below the scroll box, and click the left mouse button as many times as is necessary to move the scroll box to the bottom of the scroll bar.

The column of icons scrolls. Notice that the last icon is visible at the bottom of the window.

5. Point to the scroll arrow at the top of the scroll bar.

6. Press and hold the left mouse button until the scroll box moves to the top of the vertical scroll bar.

SCROLLING A WINDOW'S CONTENTS HORIZONTALLY

In the following steps, you will change the display size of icons and practice using the horizontal scroll bar of a window.

HANDS ON

1. Click the View pull-down menu on the Control Panel window.

2. Click Small Icons.

The icons change to a smaller size.

3. Point to the horizontal scroll bar to the right of its scroll box.

4. Click the left mouse button.

The window's contents scroll to the left as the scroll box moves to the right.

5. Point to the scroll arrow to the left of the scroll bar.

6. Press and hold the left mouse button until the scroll box moves to the left end of the horizontal scroll bar.

The window's contents scroll to the right as the box moves to the left.

CLOSING ALL OPEN WINDOWS

In the following steps, you will restore and close the currently active windows.

HANDS ON

1. Point to an empty part of the taskbar and click the right mouse button.

The taskbar shortcut menu appears.

2. Click Undo Minimize All.

The three windows you last tiled vertically open in the same arrangement on the Desktop.

3. Click the Close button on the Control Panel window.

The Control Panel window is closed and removed from the Desktop.

4. Click the Close button on the System (C:) window.

The System (C:) window is closed and removed from the Desktop.

5. Click the Close button on the My Computer window.

The My Computer window is closed and removed from the Desktop.

GETTING HELP ON SCREEN

on-screen Help A window that opens to provide contextual assistance and other learning aids.

Now that you can scroll to view window information, you are ready to use the powerful **on-screen Help** system built into Windows NT. If you don't know how to do something or forget a command, you can look it up here.

One of the Start menu choices is Help. This command displays the Help Topics: Windows NT Help window as shown in Figure 2-16.

FIGURE 2-16

The Windows NT Help window

Near the top of the Help window are three tabs: Contents, Index, and Find. These tabs represent pages. The front tab is the page that is currently open, and its contents are displayed below it. In this case, the Contents page is open, and you see Help topics in the window. If you double-click one of the topics, you either display help on that subject or a list of books contained within that book. You can double-click the desired book to display its contents. Often, more topics are available than fit on the screen. The vertical scroll bar lets you find these topics.

Clicking the Index tab allows you to see an alphabetical listing of Help topics. You can get to the desired topic quickly by typing it in the text box at the top of the Index window. When you type a letter, the display scrolls to the first topic beginning with that letter. As you continue typing, you will get closer to the topic you want. You can also use the scroll bar to find the desired topic. When you've highlighted the topic you want, press (Enter) to display the information on that subject.

The Find page lets you search for words in the description of the Help information, rather than searching by topic.

glossary term In Windows NT Help windows, a word or phrase that appears underlined with dots and can be selected to display a definition.

Figure 2-17 shows the Windows NT Help window that appears when you select the "Starting a Program" topic. You can use the vertical scroll bar to scan through the Help text. Words and phrases with dots underneath them are **glossary terms**. Your pointer changes shape when you are pointing to a

jump In Windows NT Help, a word or phrase that, when selected, immediately displays additional, related information.

glossary term; it becomes a hand pointer as shown in Figure 2-17. Clicking these words displays a definition of the word or phrase. Other words or phrases may have icons next to them. These **jumps** switch to related Help screens when you click them.

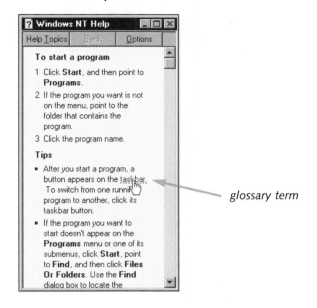

glossary term

FIGURE 2-17
The "Starting a Program" Help window

GETTING ASSISTANCE WITH WINDOWS NT HELP

In the following steps, you will practice using the Windows NT Help system.

HANDS ON

1. Click the Start button.

The Start menu appears.

2. Click Help.

The Help files load and the Help Topics: Windows NT Help window appears, as shown in Figure 2-16.

3. If necessary, click the Contents tab to display the list of topics.

4. Click the book icon labeled "How To . . . ."

The object highlights.

5. Click Open.

A set of topics appears, as shown in Figure 2-18. Notice that the Open button at the bottom of the Help window changes to Close.

6. Click the Run Programs book icon.

The object highlights.

7. Click Open.

A set of subtopics appears.

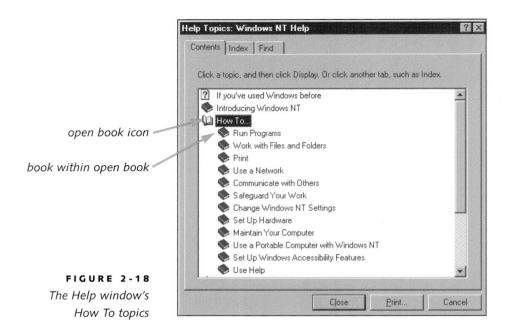

open book icon

book within open book

FIGURE 2-18
*The Help window's
How To topics*

8. Click the document icon labeled "Starting a Program."

The object highlights, and the Close button changes to Display.

9. Click Display.

A Windows NT Help window appears with a set of numbered procedures for starting applications programs. Notice that the Help Topics window is removed from the Desktop.

10. Scroll the information in the Help window, if you cannot see it all.

11. Click Help Topics.

The Help Topics: Windows NT Help window appears.

USING THE WINDOWS NT HELP INDEX

In the following steps, you will use the Windows NT Help index.

**HANDS
ON**

1. Make sure the Help Topics: Windows NT Help window is open on the Desktop.

2. Click the Index tab.

The Windows NT Help set of index topics appears, as shown in Figure 2-19. Notice that a blinking insertion bar appears in the text box for item 1.

3. Type **printing**.

As you type letters, the list of Help topics scrolls in the item 2 scroll box. A set of printing topics appears.

4. Click the subtopic labeled "documents."

The subtopic highlights.

FIGURE 2-19

The Windows Help index

5. Click the Display button.

A Windows NT Help window appears with information on printing documents.

6. Click Help Topics.

The Windows Help Contents appears.

FINDING HELP INFORMATION

In the following steps, you will practice using the Windows NT Help Find feature.

HANDS ON

1. Make sure the Windows Help Contents is visible in the Windows NT Help window.

2. Click the Find tab.

The Find Setup Wizard may appear, as shown in Figure 2-20.

N O T E   *If the Find Setup Wizard box does not appear, click the Rebuild button.*

This box lets you select how large a list Windows will search. *Minimize Database Size (recommended)* creates a shorter list, using less hard disk space. *Maximize Search Capabilities* uses more disk space, but permits the most thorough search. *Custom Search Capabilities* can create a more limited (and smaller) list to your specifications.

3. Click Next.

Another box appears with a Finish button.

FIGURE 2-20
The Find Setup Wizard

4. Click Finish.

Wait while Windows NT creates its terms list and displays your Find options.

5. Type **cascade**.

The characters appear in the text box, and a list of topics appears in the item 3 scroll box.

6. Make sure the topic "To Display All Open Windows" is selected.

7. Click Display.

A Windows NT Help window appears with information on the selected topic.

8. Click the Close button.

9. If you want to quit your work on the computer, click the Start button, click Shut Down, and log off.

LESSON SUMMARY AND EXERCISES

After you complete this lesson, you should know how to do the following:

WORKING WITH WINDOWS

- Identify the elements within windows, such as the title bar and the menu bar.

POSITIONING AND SIZING WINDOWS

- Move windows to new positions on the Desktop by clicking on the title bar and dragging to a new location.

- Change the size and shape of a window by dragging the window borders.

ARRANGING MULTIPLE WINDOWS WITH THE TASKBAR MENU

- Use the Cascade Windows option to display the title bars of all open windows simultaneously.

- Use the Tile Windows options to display the contents of all open windows simultaneously.

ARRANGING ICONS

- Drag icons to new locations within a window or on the Desktop.

- Neatly organize the icons within a window or on the Desktop by clicking the right mouse button and selecting the Arrange Icons option.

USING SCROLL BARS

- Use the scroll bars to bring contents that are out of view in a window into view.

GETTING HELP ON SCREEN

- Find Help on any Windows NT topic by clicking the Start button and selecting the Help option.

- Display definitions of Windows NT terms by clicking them in a Help window.

NEW TERMS TO REMEMBER

After you complete this lesson, you should know the meaning of these terms:

active window	maximize	size
cascade	menu bar	small icon
control menu icon	minimize	tile
glossary term	on-screen Help	title bar
horizontal scroll bar	restore	toggle
inactive window	scroll arrow	vertical scroll bar
jump	scroll bar	
large icon	scroll box	

MATCHING EXERCISE

Match each of the terms with the definitions on the right:

TERMS	DEFINITIONS
1. cascade	**a.** Standard window element on the right end of title bars that reduces a window to a button on the taskbar
2. control menu icon	
3. document window	**b.** Windows NT command that arranges all open windows on the Desktop so that each is in view and occupies the same amount of screen area
4. Maximize button	
5. menu bar	
6. Minimize button	**c.** The window that you are currently using; the one with the colored title bar
7. active window	
8. scroll bar	**d.** Standard element in application windows, generally located near the top of the window and below the title bar, that contains pull-down menu names
9. tile	
10. title bar	
	e. Standard window element that allows the contents of a window to be brought into view, either vertically or horizontally
	f. Standard window element that is at the top of every window and that contains a set of icons or buttons for controlling the size and placement of a window
	g. Standard window element on the right end of title bars that enlarges a window to full-screen size
	h. Specific type of window that displays information within an application window
	i. Standard Windows icon that appears on the left end of title bars and that displays a menu for controlling the size and placement of the window as well as closing the window or switching to another application window
	j. Windows command that arranges all open windows on the Desktop so that they overlap, with the active window in front

COMPLETION EXERCISE

Fill in the missing word or phrase for each of the following:

1. All of the work that you do in Windows NT takes place inside of a(n)

_____.

2. To view information that exists below the last visible line at the bottom of a document window, you can use the

_____.

3. A(n) _____ is a screen element that can be dragged to bring information into view in a window or list, and it represents the approximate location of the visible information in the document or list.

4. Click the _____ to enlarge a window to fill the Desktop.

5. The _____ command arranges open windows in a stack with small portions of open windows visible.

6. In Windows NT Help windows _____ can be clicked to display definitions.

7. A menu option that alternately turns on and off each time you select it is called a(n) _____.

8. A pull-down menu appears when you click a name on the _____ in an application window.

9. If you want to keep an application window available but out of the way while working with another application or feature, you can reduce its window to a taskbar button by clicking the

_____.

10. The _____ on a full-screen window's title bar returns the window to the size it was before it was maximized.

SHORT-ANSWER QUESTIONS

Write a brief answer to each of the following questions:

1. List at least five objects or elements that are common to both application and document windows.

2. Differentiate between maximizing, minimizing, and restoring a window.

3. List and describe briefly the three types of pointers that let you change the size of a window.

4. Describe briefly the advantages and disadvantages of the Cascade Windows and Tile Windows commands for arranging information on the Desktop.

5. List and describe briefly the purpose of the four elements on a scroll bar that you can use for scrolling information.

6. What is the purpose of on-screen Help?

7. Define jump.

8. Why don't all windows have a Restore button?

9. When multiple windows are open, how do you identify the active window?

10. What is a toggle command?

APPLICATION PROJECTS

Perform the following actions to complete these projects:

1. Open the My Computer window. Open the Control Panel window, activate the My Computer window, and then open the Printers Folder window. Point to an empty area of the taskbar, and click the right mouse button to display its shortcut menu. Select Cascade Windows. Activate each window separately by clicking any visible part of an inactive window. Display the taskbar shortcut menu twice more to select Tile Windows Horizontally and then Tile Windows Vertically. Practice activating windows in each arrangement, and then close all of the open windows.

2. Select Help on the taskbar Start button menu to load the Windows NT Help system. Open the topic, "Tips and Tricks," and then select the subtopics "For Maintaining Your Computer" and "Checking Your Hard Disk Drive For Errors." Does the Help window that appears contain a glossary term? If so, what is the term? Display and read its definition. Close the Help window.

3. Use the Help window's Find page to see if you can locate the following terms: "embed," "folder," and "drag." How many could you find? If you find any, display and read the information that contains these terms.

4. Double-click the My Computer icon. Use the dragging technique to size the window so that it occupies about half the horizontal Desktop area. Click the My Computer window's Maximize button, and then click its Restore button. Close the My Computer window.

5. Double-click the Recycle Bin icon. Use the dragging technique to reposition the window in the lower-right corner of the Desktop. Next, select the Recycle Bin window's control menu and click Close. If you are finished working, log off the computer.

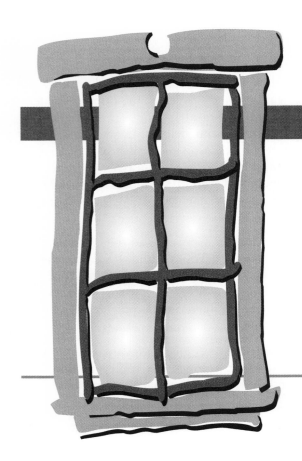

INVESTIGATING YOUR COMPUTER

OBJECTIVES

After you complete this lesson, you will be able to do the following:

- *Recognize the types and drive letters of the storage devices attached to your computer.*

- *Distinguish among system, program, and document files.*

- *Search through the contents of disk drives.*

- *Use the Control Panel to examine the hardware resources of your computer.*

- *Expand and collapse the display of hardware devices and their properties.*

- *View the settings and capabilities of your printer.*

CONTENTS

Opening the My Computer Window

Examining System Properties

Exploring Hardware Devices

Using the Printers Folder

To work on the same project from one day to the next, your computer stores or saves collections of information from one computing session to another. Files contain the data that you, the operating system, and the application software need to perform any task. Modern computing systems have thousands of files. The Windows NT 4.0 operating system alone consists of hundreds of files. With so many files, it is important to keep them organized for efficient use.

This lesson teaches you about this file organization and gives you hands-on instructions to locate and display the files stored on your computer. Here, you will investigate your computer system to learn how it organizes and displays information.

OPENING THE MY COMPUTER WINDOW

file A named, ordered collection of information stored on a disk.

Each named, ordered collection of information stored on a disk is called a **file**. The My Computer Desktop icon lets you find information about the devices and files that make up your computer system. You will open this icon to examine your disk storage system, and your printer and hardware settings. Double-clicking this icon displays a window like the one shown in Figure 3-1. Since this information is computer-specific, your window will probably contain icons different from this figure. Lesson 3 concentrates on the items found on most computer systems.

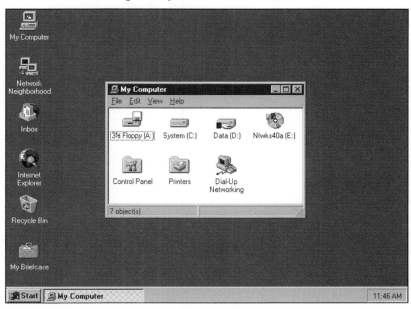

FIGURE 3-1
The My Computer window

STORAGE DEVICES

The My Computer window displays an icon for each of the storage devices attached to your computer system. Below each of these device icons is the alphabetical letter followed by a colon used to identify that device. Table 3-1 lists the most common storage devices and the device icons that represent them.

TABLE 3-1:   **STORAGE DEVICE ICONS**

ICON	DEVICE TYPE
	Floppy disk drives
	Hard, or fixed, disk drives not shared
	Shared or network drive
	CD-ROM drive

Your top or leftmost floppy disk drive is usually assigned drive letter *A:*. If you have a second floppy disk drive, it should be labeled *B:*. Your primary hard disk drive is *C:*. Additional hard disk drives, tape drives, CD-ROM drives, and so on, have their own letters. If you are connected to other storage devices via a network, these devices are also represented by icons and letters. The hand that seems to be holding the disk drive means that the drive is shared. A **shared drive** is one that can be accessed by other users of this computer or other users of the network.

shared drive A storage device that can be used by other users of the computer or network.

FILES

system files The files that operate the computer.

program files Files that let you perform tasks on the computer.

document files Files that store the work you have done with the computer.

file icon A small image that represents a specific type of named data on screen.

Three basic kinds of files exist: system files, program files, and document files. **System files** are the files that collectively make up your Windows NT operating system. **Program files** are the application software that you use to perform tasks on your computer. **Document files** (or data files) are the work that you create using your computer. Each different file type has its own characteristic **file icons**.

Table 3-2 shows a few of the file icons you will see on your computer.

TABLE 3-2:   **FILE ICONS**

ICON	FILE TYPE
	Files that control the operations of the computer
	Application software files
	Text document files
	Sound document files
	Picture document files

FILE WINDOWS

application window A rectangle on the Desktop containing an application's menus and document(s).

document window A rectangle within an application window for viewing and working on a document.

Two types of windows exist: application windows and document windows. **Application windows** appear when you run a program. **Document windows** let you perform separate jobs within an application window. For example, to type a letter you would open a word processing program application window. To work with several letters, you would open a document window for each letter.

FOLDERS

folder A named icon that contains files and other folders.

Storage disks contain files and folders. A **folder** is a container that you can use to organize files. An organized hard disk drive contains many folders. Each application software program creates one or more folders for its own use.

A few folder icons, such as the Printers and Control Panel folders inside the My Computer window are specially designed. The pictures on these folder icons tell you that these are not ordinary folders containing files and other folders. Rather, these special folders are part of the Windows NT 4.0 operating system. Some folders appear to be held by a hand. These folders are **shared folders**. Like shared drives, shared folders can be accessed by other users of this computer or other users on the network.

shared folder A folder that can be used by other users of the computer or network.

directory An earlier term for *folder.*

subdirectory An earlier term for a *subfolder.*

subfolder A folder nested within another folder.

Folders were called **directories** in previous versions of Windows. Folders inside of folders were called **subdirectories**. Following this convention, some Windows NT users call these nested folders **subfolders**.

VIEWING THE CONTENTS OF YOUR HARD DISK

In the following steps, you will open the My Computer window and view the contents of your hard disk.

**HANDS
ON**

1. Log on to the Windows NT operating system, if necessary.

2. Double-click the My Computer icon.

The My Computer window appears.

3. Double-click the drive C: icon.

A window appears, displaying the contents of drive C:, as shown in Figure 3-2.

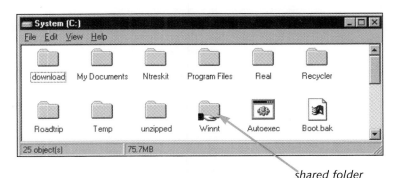

FIGURE 3-2

A drive C: window

shared folder

N O T E   *Your drive C: window will probably contain different items.*

4. If necessary, scroll the contents of the window until you can see the Winnt folder.

5. Double-click the Winnt folder.

The Winnt folder window appears on the Desktop, on top of the other open windows. It contains the Windows NT operating system files, as shown in Figure 3-3.

FIGURE 3-3
The Winnt folder

N O T E   *Your Winnt folder may display different objects.*

6. Maximize the Winnt folder. Notice the difference in shape between the folder icons and the various file icons.

7. Double-click the Help folder.

Although it may not be obvious from their files name, the Help folder contains the icons of the files that produce the on-screen Help system you used in Lesson 2. Your Help folder may display different objects from the ones shown in Figure 3.4.

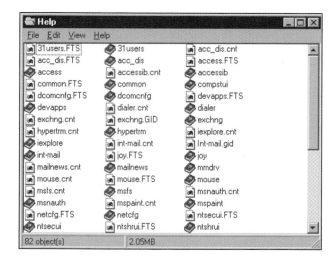

FIGURE 3-4
The Help folder

8. Examine the taskbar.

It contains a button for each window that you have opened.

9. Display the taskbar shortcut menu. (Point to a blank part of the taskbar, and click the right mouse button.)

The taskbar menu appears.

10. Choose Minimize All Windows.

All open windows reduce to clear the Desktop, but their buttons remain on the taskbar so that you can restore individual windows.

11. Click the taskbar button labeled My Computer.

The My Computer window is restored to its previous size.

VIEWING THE CONTENTS OF A FLOPPY DISK

In the following steps, you will use the Student Data Disk that comes with this book. First, you will open windows to view the contents of the floppy disk. Then you will remove the disk from the disk drive and observe the disk drive window.

HANDS ON

1. Insert your Student Data Disk into drive A: (or drive B:).

2. If your Student Data Disk is in drive A:, double-click the drive A: icon in the My Computer window; if your Student Data Disk is in drive B:, double-click the drive B: icon.

A window appears that displays the contents of your Student Data Disk, as shown in Figure 3-5.

FIGURE 3-5
The Student Data Disk window

3. Scroll to examine the unseen contents of your Student Data Disk.

4. Double-click the **Worksheets** folder.

A window appears that displays the contents of the Worksheets folder. Notice that floppy disks also use folders to organize files.

5. Close the Worksheets and Student Data Disk windows.

The My Computer window is active on the Desktop.

6. Remove your Student Data Disk from drive A: (or drive B:).

Your floppy disk drive should be empty.

7. Open the drive icon in the My Computer window that you used in step 2 above.

A warning box such as the one in Figure 3-6 appears, alerting you that your drive does not contain a disk. You will see this warning if you try to use a floppy disk without a disk in the floppy drive.

FIGURE 3-6
Warning box,
empty floppy drive

8. Insert your Student Data Disk in the floppy drive.

9. Click the Retry button.

Wait while the disk loads and its contents appear in the Floppy window.

10. Close all windows—active and inactive.

EXAMINING SYSTEM PROPERTIES

system properties Settings that affect the overall operation of your computer and the devices connected to it.

The Control Panel window is shown in Figure 3-7. Later you will have an opportunity to learn more about some of these programs, but for now, you will continue the discovery of your computer system by examining your **system properties**, or system configuration settings.

FIGURE 3-7
The Control Panel window

THE SYSTEM PROPERTIES DIALOG BOX

Double-clicking the System icon in the Control Panel window displays the System Properties dialog box, as shown in Figure 3-8. There are six index tabs in this dialog box: General, Environment, Startup/Shutdown, User Profiles, Hardware Profiles, and Performance. You click a tab to display the information you wish to see.

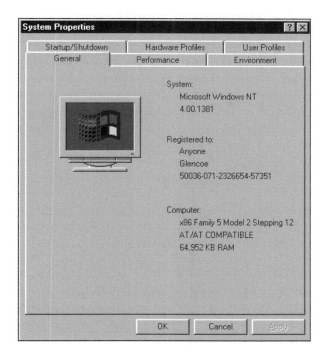

FIGURE 3-8

The System Properties
dialog box

The General tab displays the version of the Windows NT operating system used to boot your computer, the amount of memory (RAM) you have, the type of processor (CPU) running your computer, and who registers the software. The General tab only displays information; you do not set options here.

VIEWING SYSTEM PROPERTIES SETTINGS

You have already learned how to locate the System Properties dialog box from the My Computer icon. These steps show you how to use the Start menu to open the same System Properties dialog box and view option settings.

The System Properties dialog box may contain options that you do not understand. Here you will also learn how to use Windows NT to obtain on-screen contextual help.

WARNING

Your goal here is to examine the settings, not to change them. If you change System Properties inappropriately, your system might operate poorly, or not at all.

HANDS ON

1. Click the taskbar Start button.

   The Start menu appears.

2. Point to Settings.

   The Settings menu pops up.

3. Click Control Panel.

   The Control Panel window appears on the Desktop.

4. Double-click the System icon.

   The System Properties dialog box appears.

5. Click the General tab.

   Your screen should resemble Figure 3-8.

6. Click the Help button, the question mark to the left of the Close button in the Systems Properties dialog box.

The mouse pointer changes shape to become a Help pointer, an arrow with a question mark. Clicking the Help pointer onto an item on the screen displays a brief definition or explanation about that item. Clicking a second time closes the Help window.

7. Click the center of the word "Registered" in Registered to.

The Help window displayed in Figure 3-9 appears.

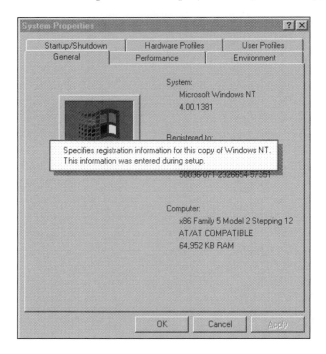

FIGURE 3-9
"Registered to" Help window

N O T E   *If the window does not appear and the pointer does not return to its regular shape, you did not click the center of the word Registered. Click the Help button and try again.*

8. Use the Help pointer to learn more about the other information in the General tab of the System Properties dialog box.

9. Click the Performance tab.

The Performance options appear in the System Properties dialog box.

10. Click the Help button and then click the word Virtual in the center of the dialog box (not the button in its lower-right corner).

The Help window on virtual memory appears.

11. Click outside the Help window to close it.

12. Click the Change button on the right side of the dialog box.

virtual memory Hard disk space used by the operating system as if it were additional main memory.

The Virtual Memory dialog box appears. **Virtual memory** is space on the hard disk drive that Windows NT uses when more main memory is needed.

13. Click the Cancel button on the Virtual Memory dialog box.

The dialog box is removed from the Desktop.

14. Close the System Properties dialog box.

The dialog box is removed from the Desktop. The Control Panel window is now active.

15. Close the Control Panel window.

The Desktop is cleared.

EXPLORING HARDWARE DEVICES

You can use the Control Panel to view and change the properties of other hardware devices on your computer or network. You can even add new devices. There are icons to control the keyboard, mouse, display, and other hardware settings.

MULTIMEDIA DEVICES

The Multimedia icon lets you see how the audio and video works on your computer. Specific information about the CD-ROM and sound card in your computer is listed in the Devices window, as shown in Figure 3-10.

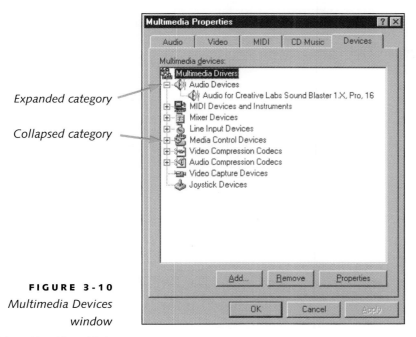

Expanded category

Collapsed category

FIGURE 3-10
Multimedia Devices window

tree A branching, hierarchical list that looks like the spreading branches or roots of a tree.

collapsed A state of an item in which details or subordinate items are hidden from view. A plus sign (+) in the box to the left of the item indicates the item is collapsed. Compare with *expanded.*

Multimedia devices connected to the system appear in a **tree**, a structured list whose branches display and hide their contents as commanded. At the top of the list is the heading Multimedia Drivers. Categories of multimedia drivers are indented below this level. The square to the left of some categories contain either a plus sign (+) or a minus sign (-). These symbols indicate the amount of detail listed on the screen. A plus sign refers to a **collapsed** level. This means that you can display specific devices for a category that are

expanded A state of an item in which details or subordinate items are visible. A minus sign (-) in the box to the left of the item indicates the item is expanded. Compare with *collapsed*.

currently hidden from view. To see (expand) the category, simply click the plus sign (+). When a category expands, its square displays a minus sign (-); this represents an **expanded** level. When a level is expanded, you can see all of the devices contained in that category. Items that do not have a box to their left do not contain any levels within them. Therefore, they cannot be expanded or collapsed.

While comprehensive descriptions of hardware devices and drivers are beyond the scope of this text, you can use the Control Panel icons to view information about almost any device by selecting the Properties button.

VIEWING MULTIMEDIA PROPERTIES

Your CD-ROM and sound card control the video and audio capabilities of your computer system. They are usually set correctly when the hardware is initially installed. The following steps let you view these settings.

WARNING

Once again, your goal here is to examine the settings, not to change them. If you change the multimedia device properties, your system may not run audio or video files properly.

1. Open the Control Panel.

2. Double-click the Multimedia icon.

The Multimedia Properties window appears as shown in Figure 3-11.

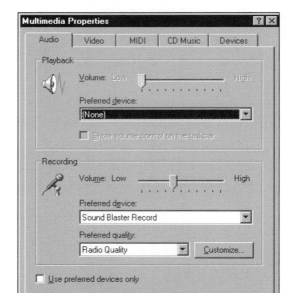

FIGURE 3-11
The Multimedia Properties dialog box

3. Click the Devices tab.

You see the categories of device drivers similar to that shown in Figure 3-10.

4. Click the plus sign (+) beside the Audio Devices category.

The category expands to show the audio device(s) within your system. Note that there is now a minus sign (-) beside Audio Devices, indicating that the category has been expanded.

5. Click Audio Device.

6. Click the Properties button.

The General properties of the Audio Device appear within a window.

7. Click the Settings button.

More detail information appears as shown in Figure 3-12. This information lets you know how your audio card recognizes and produces sound output. Your sound card will probably show different values in the configuration window.

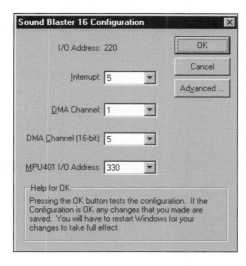

FIGURE 3-12

The Settings windows for a sound card

8. Click the Cancel button in the Configuration window.

9. Click the Cancel button in the Audio Device Properties window.

10. Click the minus sign (-) to collapse the Audio Devices category.

The minus sign changes to a plus sign indicating the category has hidden details that can be expanded.

11. Click the Cancel button in the Multimedia Properties window.

12. Close the Control Panel.

THE PRINTERS FOLDER

For easy access, Windows NT sometimes lets you run a program from more than one location. Thus, you can access the Printers folder from either the My Computer or the Control Panel windows. Double-clicking either icon displays the Printers window; an example is shown in Figure 3-13.

In this window you can select and set up the printer where you want to send your output. The Printers window contains a printer icon for each of the printer drivers installed on your system. A **printer driver** is a program file that controls or regulates a specific printer. The Printers window also

printer driver A program that regulates the operation of a specific printer model and in Windows NT is represented by a device icon.

FIGURE 3-13

The Printers window

shared printer A printer that can be used by other users of the computer or network.

wizard An automated process that guides you through an operation by presenting a series of options from which you can select.

contains an Add Printer icon, which allows you to add (install) a new printer to your system. Printers which seem to be held by a hand are shared printers. **Shared printers** can be used by other users of this computer or users of the network.

You can easily and simply add many devices to your computer system. Printers are installed through the Add Printer Wizard dialog box shown in Figure 3-14. A **wizard** is an automated process that guides you through an operation with which you may be unfamiliar. If Windows NT knows the printer, the installation process needs only the Windows NT disk; if Windows NT does not know the printer, the manufacturer of the printer will supply the driver files.

FIGURE 3-14

The first Add Printer Wizard dialog box

When you double-click a printer icon, a status window appears with the name of the specific printer model on its title bar. Any output being printed appears in this window, as shown in Figure 3-15.

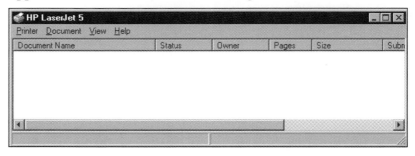

FIGURE 3-15

The status window for a printer

Settings for a specific printer can be modified via its Properties dialog box. The name of your printer model appears on the title bar. There are two ways to access this dialog box. You can highlight the printer's device icon in the Printers window and then select Properties on the File menu. Alternatively, you can open the printer's status window, select the Printer menu on the menu bar, and select Properties. The Properties window for each printer is a multi-tabbed dialog box similar to the one shown in Figure 3-16.

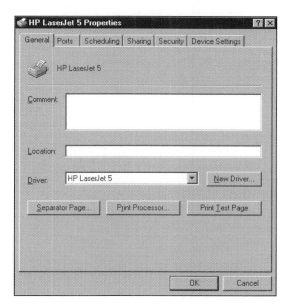

FIGURE 3-16
*The Properties dialog box
for a printer*

You will learn much more about controlling your printer in a later lesson.

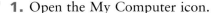

VIEWING PRINTER SETTINGS

In the following steps, you will open the Printers window and view the current print settings for the printer connected to your system.

**HANDS
ON**

1. Open the My Computer icon.

2. Open the Printers folder.

3. Click the device icon for the printer connected to your system to highlight that icon.

4. Choose Properties from the File menu.

The Properties dialog box appears. Notice that its title bar displays your printer's model name.

5. One at a time, click each of the tabs on your printer's Properties dialog box to view the different categories of information for your printer. Use the Help pointer to learn about any options you find unclear.

6. Close the Properties dialog box.

7. Click the Close button in the My Computer window.

8. If you wish to end your computing session, follow the instructions in your lab, or log off your computer according to the directions in Lesson 1. Otherwise, proceed to the exercises that conclude this lesson.

LESSON SUMMARY AND EXERCISES

After you complete this lesson, you should know how to do the following:

OPENING THE MY COMPUTER WINDOW

- Identify the objects on your computer, including files, devices, and icons.
- Use the My Computer icon to find out about the storage devices and other objects on your computer.
- Display the folders and files located on the hard disk attached to your computer.
- View the contents of a floppy disk.

EXAMINING SYSTEM PROPERTIES

- Display the general properties of your computer system.

EXPLORING HARDWARE DEVICES

- View the properties of the multimedia devices on your computer.

USING THE PRINTERS FOLDER

- View the settings of the printer(s) attached to your system.

NEW TERMS TO REMEMBER

After you complete this lesson, you should know the meaning of these terms:

application window	shared drive
collapsed	shared folder
directory	shared printer
document files	subdirectory
document window	subfolder
expanded	system files
file	system properties
file icon	tree
folder	virtual memory
printer driver	wizard
program file	

MATCHING EXERCISE

Match each of the terms with the definitions on the right:

TERMS	DEFINITIONS
1. document file	**a.** Storage used by the operating system as if it were main memory
2. drive icon	
3. file icon	**b.** A container for files and other icons
4. folder	**c.** The software that regulates the operation of your printer
5. virtual memory	**d.** The branch of a storage device tree, labeled (–), that shows its components
6. expanded	
7. program file	**e.** Icon that represents a storage device and that activates a window that displays the files and folders stored on the device
8. system files	
9. printer driver	**f.** Files that operate the computer
10. wizard	**g.** An automatic process that guides you through a series of complex steps
	h. Files that contain instructions used by application software
	i. On-screen picture that represents information named and stored in a specific location
	j. Named set of data that is created while working with an application and stored in a specific location

COMPLETION EXERCISE

Fill in the missing word or phrase for each of the following:

1. In the device tree structure displayed on the Multimedia Properties window, you can click a plus sign (+) to _____ the level.

2. Each named, ordered collection of information stored on a disk is called a(n) _____.

3. The first hard disk on your computer is named the _____ drive.

4. System configuration settings are called _____.

5. If you use a word processing application to type a memo, the text that makes up the memo is stored in a(n) _____.

6. On the tree structure of devices in the Multimedia Properties drivers window, a minus sign (–) represents an object that is _____.

7. A storage device, folder, or printer that can be used by others on a network is said to be _____.

8. A(n)_____ is an automated process that guides the user through an unfamiliar operation.

9. The _____ allows you to display a brief definition or an explanation about an on-screen item.

10. The _____ is a program file that controls or regulates a specific printer.

SHORT-ANSWER QUESTIONS

Write a brief answer to each of the following questions:

1. How do you use the Windows NT contextual Help system?

2. What would happen if your computer only had files, but no folders?

3. List the three major file categories and the purpose of each.

4. What happens if you try to open a floppy drive icon without a disk in the drive?

5. What steps should you take to remedy the problem described in question 4?

6. Why does Windows NT have property windows?

7. What is a subfolder?

8. Why does each printer need a printer driver?

9. Some dialog boxes appear in a tree. How do you use this structure?

10. From the information presented in this lesson, how could you find out the version of the Windows NT operating system you are using?

APPLICATION PROJECTS

Perform the following actions to complete these projects:

1. Display the Keyboard icon located in the Control Panel. Use contextual Help to learn more about your keyboard settings. (Do not change any settings.) Close all open windows.

2. Suppose you were able to purchase a new modem. List the steps, in logical order, you would expect to perform to install the device properly. Be precise.

3. Display the settings for the modem connected to your computer or network. Use contextual Help to learn more about the properties of your modem. (Do not change any settings.)

4. Display the settings for the mouse connected to your computer or network. Use contextual Help to learn more about the properties of your mouse. (Do not change any settings.)

5. Windows 95 has a feature known as Plug and Play. With this feature, the operating system automatically detects and installs new hardware. Compare this feature with the way Windows NT 4.0 installs new hardware.

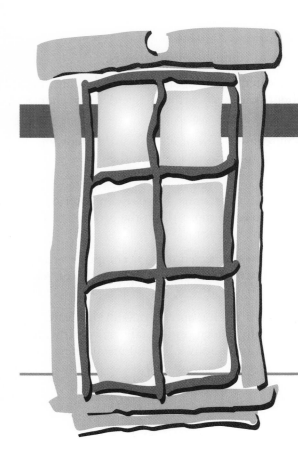

LESSON 4

EXPLORING

DISK

ORGANIZATION

OBJECTIVES

After you complete this lesson, you will be able to do the following:

- *Use the Windows NT Explorer to view and modify the structure of a disk.*

- *Modify the appearance of the Exploring window.*

- *Format a disk to prepare it to store information.*

- *Create folders and subfolders on a disk.*

- *Rename, delete, copy, and move folders.*

- *Design folder structures that suit different needs.*

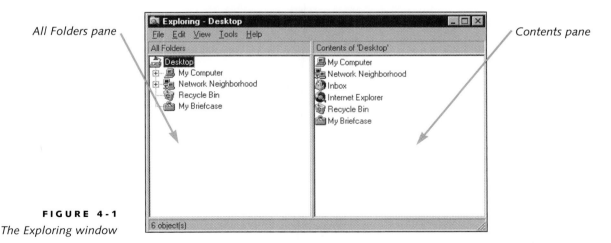

nformation is the computer's most important product. As a computer user, you must be able to locate and use stored information and to save ongoing work for future use. Protecting and updating that information requires careful organization by the operating system. Data must be stored properly so that it can be found later.

In Lesson 3 you learned that the file is the basic unit of disk storage; all the information that you store is in the form of files. In this lesson, you will use the Windows NT Explorer to analyze the organization of your hard disk and then apply that knowledge to the organization of a new floppy disk.

USING THE WINDOWS NT EXPLORER

The Windows NT Explorer opens to display its Exploring window. Resembling the My Computer window, the Exploring window lets you search through your computer's storage system to examine its contents and organization. Figure 4-1 shows the Exploring window with all its components collapsed.

All Folders pane

Contents pane

FIGURE 4-1
The Exploring window

Like the other windows that you have seen, the Exploring window is headed by its title bar, with its menu bar just beneath. Below the title bar and the menu bar, the Explorer window divides vertically into two sections or (window) **panes**: All Folders and Contents.

pane A bordered area within a window.

THE ALL FOLDERS PANE

On the left side of the Exploring window is the All Folders pane. It shows a tree of folders that displays the hierarchical organization of available disks. One of the icons in the All Folders pane is the selected object. Its name appears in the window's title bar, becoming Exploring - Desktop in Figure 4-1.

The root or base of the entire Windows NT tree is the Desktop. Exploring - Desktop displays the Desktop icon at the top of the All Folders pane, with each icon Windows NT places on the Desktop listed below. Since the purpose of the Exploring window is to display the contents of all files to which you have access, you may see different icons when you explore your computer's Desktop.

Expanding a branch in the All Folders pane displays that branch's folders. Figure 4-2 shows how the All Folders pane changes by expanding the My Computer branch. Icons for the available disk drives appear along with the Control Panel and Printers system folders.

My Computer folder

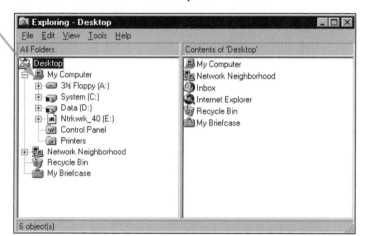

FIGURE 4-2
The Exploring window with My Computer expanded

Although each drive icon has the shape of the drive it represents, each drive icon is also a main or top-level folder. Each **main folder** can hold files and subfolders. The main folder is also called the **root directory**.

NOTE

In spite of the technical distinction between a main folder and its subfolders, many people refer to them both as folders.

main folder The top level of a disk icon, which contains files and folders that are not nested within any other folder; also referred to as the root directory.

Figure 4-3 shows how the All Folders pane changes by expanding the System (C:) branch. Notice that some folder levels display a plus sign (+) and some do not. The plus sign tells you that the folder contains one or more other folders (or subfolders). Folders without a plus sign are empty or contain only files.

THE CONTENTS PANE

The Contents pane on the right side of the Exploring window displays the contents of the object selected in the All Folders pane. In Figures 4-1, 4-2, and 4-3, the Contents pane does not change, because the Desktop is the selected object in each figure. Figure 4-4 shows the Exploring window with System (C:) selected. Compare the title bar and Contents pane of Figure 4-4 with Figure 4-3. The Contents pane in Figure 4-4 shows icons of the objects contained in the C: drive.

root directory An earlier name for the main folder in a disk.

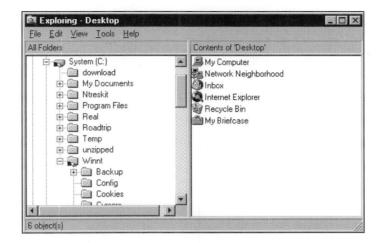

FIGURE 4-3

The Exploring window with System (C:) branch

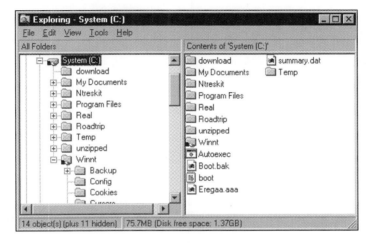

FIGURE 4-4

Exploring window with System (C:) selected—note change in Contents pane

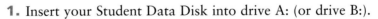

EXPLORE YOUR HARD DISK

In the following steps, you will open the Exploring window, select various objects, and expand and collapse several folders to view the hierarchical structure of your hard disk. Begin with your computer on and booted with the Windows NT 4.0 operating system.

HANDS ON

1. Insert your Student Data Disk into drive A: (or drive B:).

2. Display the Start menu.

3. Highlight Programs and click Windows NT Explorer.

The Exploring window appears.

4. Adjust the Exploring window so that it resembles Figure 4-4.

   a. If Desktop is not the top object in the All Folders pane, drag its vertical scroll box to the top of the scroll bar.

   b. If the description All Folders is not at the top of its pane, choose Options from the window's View menu to display the Options dialog box, as shown in Figure 4-5. Click the check box to the left of Include Description Bar For Right And Left Panes and click OK.

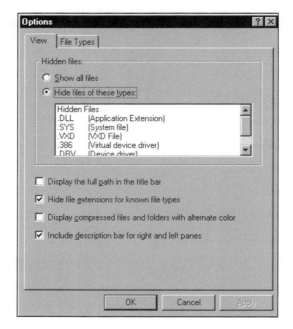

FIGURE 4-5

*The Exploring window's
Options dialog box*

c. If there is a plus sign (+) beside the My Computer icon, click the plus sign to expand its sublevels.

d. Choose List from the View menu to display objects in the Contents pane in columns.

5. Click the Winnt folder in the All Folders pane.

The title bar says "Exploring-Winnt." The Contents pane says "Contents of 'Winnt '" and displays the objects in the Winnt folder.

6. Click the My Computer icon's minus sign (–) to collapse the My Computer level.

My Computer is now selected. The title bar says "Exploring – My Computer." The drive icons and system folders appear in the Contents pane, and a plus sign (+) appears beside the My Computer icon.

7. Press ⟶.

The My Computer level in the All Folders pane expands.

N O T E   *The keyboard's left and right arrow keys can substitute for mouse clicks to expand or collapse a folder.*

8. Press ⬇ repeatedly until System (C:) highlights.

The folders and/or files in the main folder for drive C: appear in the Contents pane.

N O T E   *The keyboard's down arrow key allows you to move down the All Folders tree. Each time you press ⬇, the object just below the currently selected one highlights, the object's name appears in the Exploring title bar, and the object's contents come into view in the Contents pane.*

9. Alternating between the keyboard and the mouse, expand and collapse the various folders in the All Folders pane until you are well acquainted with the hierarchical organization of your computer system.

HINT   *When you first work with an unfamiliar computer system that runs Windows NT, the Windows NT Explorer can quickly help you to understand its file organization.*

10. Select the device icon for the disk drive that contains your Student Data Disk (drive A: or B:) in the All Folders pane.

The contents of the Student Data Disk appear in the Contents pane. Notice (in case you haven't already) that you do not need to expand a folder in the All Folders pane in order to see its details in the Contents pane.

CUSTOMIZING THE EXPLORING WINDOW

Your preliminary investigation of the Windows NT Explorer demonstrates its benefit. When you customize it, however, it becomes even more useful. The Explorer customization commands are under the View menu.

VIEW OPTIONS

Begin to customize your Exploring window by using the View menu commands, as shown in Figure 4-6. These commands are explained in Table 4-1.

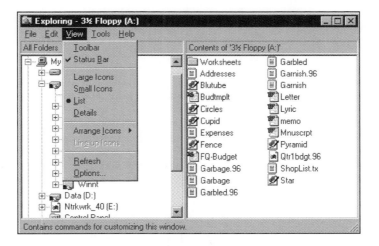

FIGURE 4-6
The Exploring window's View menu

TABLE 4-1:   EXPLORER VIEW MENU COMMANDS

OPTION	DESCRIPTION
Toolbar	Displays or hides a row of tool buttons just below the menu bar with shortcuts for common menu commands.
Status Bar	Displays or hides a bar at the bottom of the window that explains selected objects or menu commands.
Large Icons	Changes the Contents pane. A large icon appears above each folder or file name. First folders, then files, are arranged in rows and columns. Objects can be dragged to different locations.

TABLE 4-1:   **EXPLORER VIEW MENU COMMANDS, continued**

Small Icons	Changes the Contents pane. A small icon appears to the left of each folder or file name. First folders, then files, are arranged in rows and columns. Objects can be dragged to different locations.
List	Changes the Contents pane. Small icons appear to the left of folder and file names. Listing is in columns from top to bottom. Dragging an object within the pane does not change its location.
Details	Changes the Contents pane. Small icons appear to the left of folder and file names. Listing is in a single column. To the right of each file name appears the size, type, and date the file was last saved.
Arrange Icons	Lets you determine the order in which the files appear, by name, type, size, or date. Auto Arrange keeps objects aligned as you drag them around the window.
Line Up Icons	Aligns objects in columns and/or rows after you have dragged them around the window.
Refresh	Updates the information displayed in the window to reflect the most current changes.
Options	Displays an options window with two tabs. The View tab controls which files are displayed in the Contents pane. The File Types tab provides access to a list of file types and their associated icons.

CHANGING WINDOW PANE VIEWS

In the following steps, you will change several of the Exploring window's view options and observe the way the objects in the Exploring window alter.

HANDS ON

1. Begin with the Exploring window maximized and active on the Desktop. Select the System (C:) drive icon in the All Folders pane.

2. Examine the Exploring window to see if its toolbar is visible. If it is, go to the next step. If the toolbar is hidden, choose Toolbar from the View menu to display the toolbar.

The Exploring toolbar is toggled on. Figure 4-7 identifies the toolbar buttons.

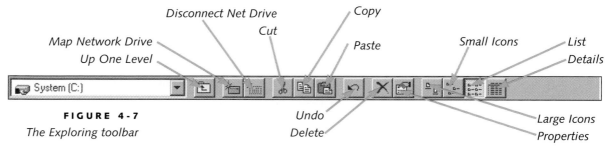

FIGURE 4-7
The Exploring toolbar

3. Display the View menu to see that the status bar is checked. If it is, click outside the menu to close it. If the status bar is not checked, click its menu choice to display the status bar near the bottom of the Exploring window.

4. Point to the View menu and then point to the Arrange menu to see its choices. If Auto Arrange is not checked, click outside the menu to close it. Otherwise, click its menu choice to toggle Auto Arrange off.

NOTE *When Auto Arrange has a check mark, Contents pane objects arrange themselves according to an invisible grid whenever you move them.*

Tool Tip Text which appears when you point to a tool and provides information about the tool.

5. Point to the Details tool, the last button on the right end of the toolbar.

A rectangle labeled "Details" appears briefly. This is a **Tool Tip**. Tool Tips help you identify individual tools on a toolbar.

6. Click the Details tool (and keep it pressed).

The Details tool looks pressed in on screen and the status bar says "Displays information about each item in the window." As you issue a command, the status bar often explains what that command does.

7. Release the mouse button.

The Details tool still looks pressed in. The Contents pane displays in **Detail view**, which lists name, size, type, and date and time modified for each object in the Contents pane.

Detail view An option for displaying objects in the Contents pane in the Exploring window, which shows the name, size, type, and date and time modified for each object in the Contents pane.

8. Modify steps 6 and 7 to press and release the List tool.

The List tool displays the Contents objects as small icons without any details.

9. Modify steps 6 and 7 to press and release the Small Icons tool.

The Small Icons tool displays the Contents objects as small icons in columns and rows.

10. Drag individual Content objects to blank places in the Contents pane.

Small Icon view lets you drag objects into custom locations in the Contents pane.

11. Modify steps 6 and 7 to press and release the Large Icons tool.

The Large Icons tool displays the Contents objects as large icons in columns and rows.

12. Drag individual Content objects to blank places in the Contents pane.

Large Icon view lets you drag objects into custom locations in the Contents pane.

13. Click the Details button to display the Contents pane in Details view.

14. Choose Arrange Icons from the View menu.

The Arrange Icons menu shown in Figure 4-8 appears beside the View menu.

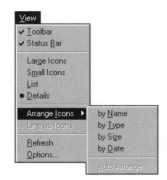

FIGURE 4-8

The Arrange Icons menu

15. Click By Date.

The Contents pane list rearranges. Objects are now organized by date (modified) from newest to oldest.

16. Click View, Arrange Icons, By Size.

The Contents pane list rearranges. Objects are now organized by file size from smallest to biggest.

17. Click View, Arrange Icons, By Type.

The Contents pane list rearranges. Objects are now organized first by file **type** and then alphabetically within each object category.

type (of icon/file) The category of information or application to which an icon or a file belongs.

18. Click the word "Name" above the names of the folders and files in the Contents pane.

The Contents pane arranges its object list into computer alphabetical order; numbers precede letters. Instead of accessing icon arrangement from the View menu, you can simply click the Name, Size, Type, Modified, and Attributes buttons near the top of the Contents pane to arrange icons accordingly.

TIP   *If you click the buttons a second time, the files will be listed in the opposite order.*

WINDOW PANES

separator line A line dividing two panes in a window, which can be dragged to make one pane larger and the other smaller.

Another way to customize the Exploring window is to move the **separator line,** the thick line that divides the window panes. Dragging the separator line left or right makes one pane wider and the other narrower. When an object such as the System (C:) folder contains several levels of subfolders, widening the All Folders pane lets you expand some or all of its branches without scrolling. When an object such as the Windows folder contains many other objects, widening the Contents pane displays more items.

SIZING EXPLORING WINDOW PANES

In the following steps, you will use your mouse to change the widths of the All Folders and Contents panes. You will also adjust the Contents pane's details columns (Name, Size, Type, Modified Attributes) to display more or less information.

HANDS ON

1. Point to the separator line between the All Folders and Contents pane.

When the pointer is in the correct location, it becomes a horizontal, double-headed arrow.

2. Drag the pointer approximately 1 inch to the left, as shown in Figure 4-9.

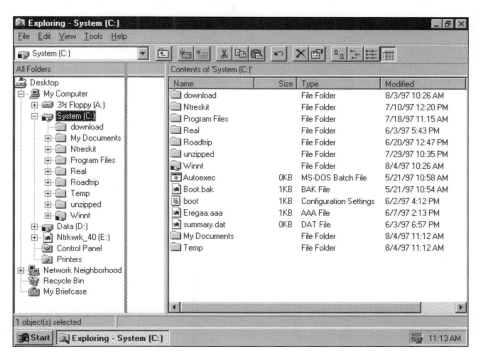

FIGURE 4-9

Moving a window pane

As you drag the mouse, a vertical line also moves, to mark the current pane location.

3. Release the mouse button.

The panes resize, as shown in Figure 4-10. Now the Contents pane has more room to display its details.

Next you will size the detail columns.

4. Point to the vertical separator line between the headings "Type" and "Modified."

5. Drag the separator line to the left approximately 1 inch.

truncated An object that is cut off, for example, by a border, so that part of it is not displayed.

The longer type descriptions are cut off or **truncated**, such as "Configurat…" in Figure 4-11. When Windows NT truncates text such as a file name or a type description, it places an ellipsis (…) at the end of the line to indicate that the entire text passage is not displayed.

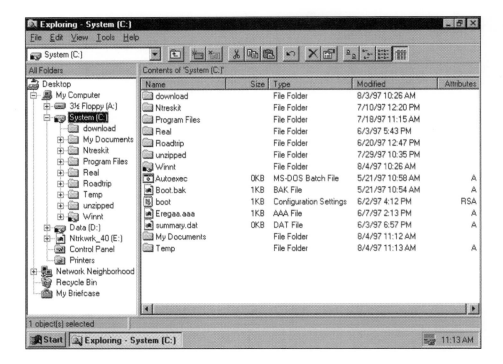

*The resized All Folders
and Contents panes*

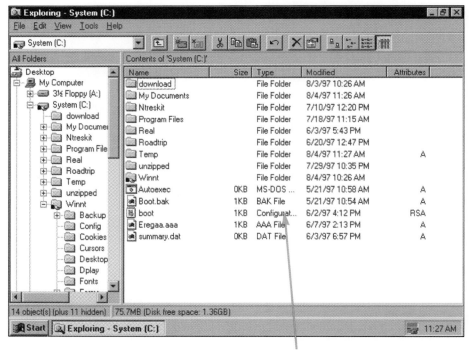

Truncated type descriptions

truncated description

6. Drag the separator line between Type and Modified to the right until you can see the entire Type column.

The file type descriptions should display fully in the Type column.

7. Close the Exploring window.

FORMATTING DISKS

formatting (1) An operating system process which removes all existing data from a disk and prepares the disk to receive new data; (2) enhancements applied within a document to make the document more readable and attractive.

file system The method used by the operating system to control access to a disk.

File Allocation Table (FAT) Disk file system that the operating system uses to read data from and write data to the disk. Used in Windows NT 4.0 to maintain compatibility with previous versions of Windows and DOS.

NT File System (NTFS) A file system new to Windows NT 4.0 that provides greater efficiency and security than the FAT file system.

Before a disk can hold files and folders, it must be formatted. The **formatting** process erases any files already stored on the disk and then copies onto the disk information that the operating system uses to read data from and write data to the disk. This information includes the size of the disk, the number of characters that each sector can hold, and the location of each file. The method used to control access to the disk is called the **file system**. There are several different kinds of file systems used by Windows NT. The two most common file systems are FAT and NTFS. Old versions of DOS and previous versions of Windows used the **File Allocation Table (FAT)** file system. **NT File System (NTFS)** is a file system new to Windows NT.

In addition to performing the tasks of any file system, NTFS stores information more efficiently than FAT. NTFS also provides greater security for stored files. Network Administrators can tightly control which users have access to individual files under NTFS. One look at the properties dialog box lets you see the major difference between FAT and NTFS. In Figure 4-12, an NTFS disk's properties dialog box includes a tab named Security. The FAT disk shown in Figure 4-13 does not have this tab. Diskettes always use the FAT method.

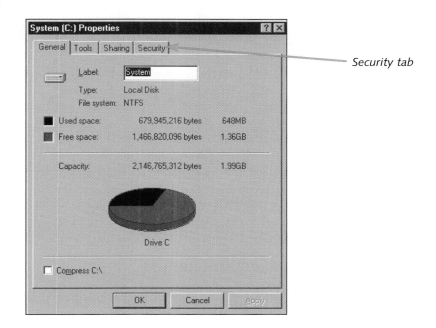

Security tab

FIGURE 4-12

Properties dialog box for an NTFS drive

The FAT contains the name of each file on the disk, as well as its size, creation date, the date the file was last modified or accessed, its type, and its location. Disks can be reformatted, but they are usually formatted only once, when they are first purchased. You can also purchase disks that have already been formatted.

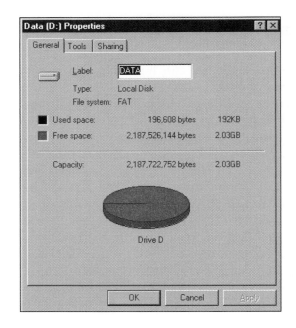

FIGURE 4-13

*Properties dialog box
for a FAT drive*

When you want to format a disk, you select the appropriate drive in the My Computer window and then select Format on the File menu. In the Format dialog box you must specify the disk drive and the capacity of the disk. Both capacity types, 5¼ inch and 3½ inch floppy disks, can be double or high density.

CAUTION   *Formatting permanently erases the information on a disk. Use care when formatting a disk to make certain you don't mistakenly format a disk containing information you want to keep.*

FORMATTING A DISK

In the following steps, you will format a blank disk.

HANDS ON

1. Obtain a blank, unformatted disk that fits the floppy disk drive that you will use to format the disk.

NOTE   *For this Hands On activity, you may use a disk that has unneeded data, if you are absolutely sure you will never want the files again. When you format a disk, you erase all data on that disk.*

2. Insert the disk into drive A: (or drive B:).

3. Double-click the My Computer icon.

The My Computer window appears on the Desktop.

4. Select the icon for the drive that contains the disk (drive A: or B:).

The icon is highlighted.

5. Choose Format from the File menu.

The Format dialog box appears. Notice that its title bar displays the type of disk drive you have selected, as shown in Figure 4-14.

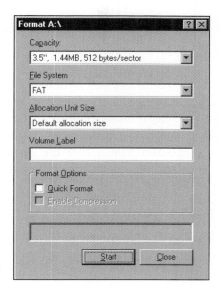

FIGURE 4-14

The Format dialog box

6. Make sure the Capacity selection matches the type of disk you have inserted in the selected drive. If it doesn't, click the drop-down arrow, and choose the correct capacity from the list.

7. Click the Volume Label text box.

An insertion point appears in the text box.

8. Type **Untitled**

9. Click Start.

A warning box appears cautioning you about formatting a disk with data on it.

10. Click OK.

As Windows NT begins the disk formatting operation, a progress bar fills from left to right. When the bar is filled, a window appears informing you that the formatting operation is finished.

NOTE   *Occasionally a disk will not format. If this happens, try to format the same disk on a different computer. If it still will not format, the disk is probably defective. Return it for a new one or throw it away.*

11. Click OK.

12. Close all open windows and dialog boxes to clear the Desktop.

CREATING FOLDERS AND SUBFOLDERS

A newly formatted disk contains no folders. Without folders, all files on the disk appear in the contents list together. When you have many files on a disk, they can become hard to keep track of. Folders allow users to organize files in a meaningful way by grouping related files together.

To create a folder, select the New command on either the shortcut menu or on the Exploring window File menu. A submenu appears. Click the Folder option and type a name for the folder. It's that simple. Use a meaningful name that describes the files you will keep in the folder.

TIP

If you don't name the folder, Windows will name it for you. The first folder will be called "New Folder," the next, "New Folder (2)," the next, "New Folder (3)," and then "New Folder (4)," "New Folder (5)," and so on.

parent folder A folder that contains one or more folders (also called subfolders).

If you wish to create a folder within a folder, you must first open the folder that will be the parent folder for the new folder. A **parent folder** is any folder that contains one or more folders. With a parent folder opened on the Desktop or in the Exploring window's All Folders or Contents pane, you can select the New command from either the shortcut menu or the Exploring window File menu, and then create the folder as previously described.

BUILDING FOLDER STRUCTURES

disk structure The organizational structure of folders and subfolders on a disk.

application-oriented structure A file management system in which subfolders within an application's folder are used to store data files created with the application. Compare with *project-oriented structure.*

Creating a meaningful folder structure requires some planning. The kind of structure you build depends on the way you use your computer and the number of people who share the information on the disk. The relationship of folders to subfolders is called the **disk structure**.

In an **application-oriented structure**, each program's folder contains one or more subfolders. For example, if your word processing program files are in a Word folder, you might create subfolders such as Memos, Letters, and so on, in the Word folder. An application-oriented structure is illustrated in Figure 4-15.

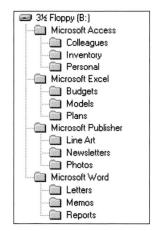

FIGURE 4-15
An application-oriented structure

project-oriented structure A file management system in which data files and folders are organized according to the specific projects. Compare with *application-oriented structure.*

user-oriented structure A file management system in which data files and folders are organized according to the individual users who share a computer or network server.

A **project-oriented structure** has separate folders for each of the tasks you do—regardless of the programs used to create those files. For example, if you were producing a newsletter, you might collect all the stories and art for the newsletter in one folder.

When more than one person uses a computer, consider a **user-oriented structure**. Here, each user saves his or her work in a separate folder. Within each personal folder, subfolders can be created and structured according to the user's needs.

In many cases, a combination of the three folder structures is used. For example, the subfolders within a user-oriented structure can be project- or application-oriented. Figure 4-16 shows examples of the different kinds of folder structures: (a) project-oriented, (b) user-oriented, and (c) combined user-application and user-project structures.

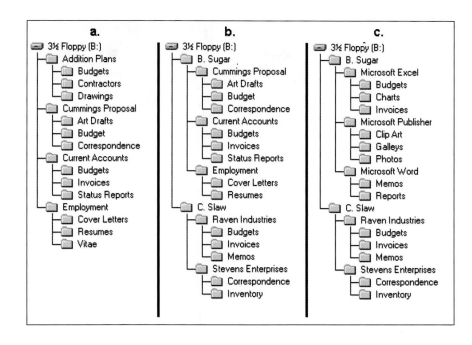

FIGURE 4-16

(a) Project-oriented,
(b) user-oriented, and
(c) combined folder
structures

CREATING FOLDERS

In the following steps, you will create two folders on your newly formatted floppy disk.

1. Open the Windows NT Explorer (under Programs in the Start menu).

TIP   *Right-click the Start button to display a shortcut menu. Click Explore to run the Windows NT Explorer.*

2. Scroll the All Folders pane to the top, if necessary.

3. Select the device icon for the disk drive that contains the disk you just formatted.

4. Click New from the File menu.

The New menu appears, allowing you to choose between Folder and Shortcut.

5. Click Folder.

A new folder icon labeled "New Folder" appears in the root directory on the blank disk in the selected drive, as shown in Figure 4-17. The icon label is highlighted, ready for you to type a name for the folder.

6. Type **Worksheets** and press Enter.

The new folder is created, named, and placed in the main folder of the disk in the specified floppy disk drive.

7. Repeat steps 3-5.

The name of the newly created folder is selected so you can type a name.

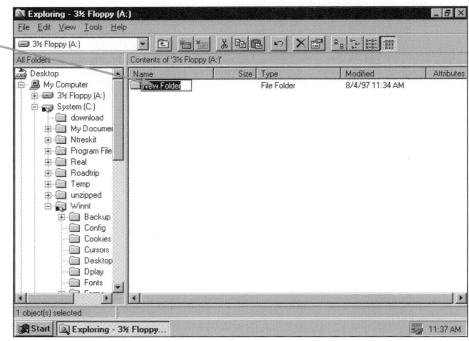

FIGURE 4-17
The "New Folder" icon

8. Type **Documents** and press [Enter].

Now you have two folders, Documents and Worksheets, in the main folder of your floppy disk.

CREATING A SUBFOLDER

In the following steps, you will create a subfolder, one folder nested within another.

HANDS ON

1. In the All Folders pane of the Exploring window, expand the device icon for the disk drive that holds your floppy disk.

Icons for the two folders you created appear in the All Folders pane.

2. Select the **Documents** folder in the All Folders pane.

The All Folders pane displays an open folder icon next to Documents. On screen, there are three indicators that the Documents folder has no contents:

■ No plus or minus sign next to the Documents icon in the All Folders pane

■ The empty Contents pane

■ 0 objects, 0 bytes in the status bar

3. Click New and then Folder from the File menu.

The New Folder icon appears in the Contents pane, the All Folders Documents folder acquires a plus sign, and the status bar says "1 object(s)."

4. Type **Toss** and press [Enter].

The new folder is created and placed *inside* the Documents folder on the disk in the specified floppy disk drive, as shown in Figure 4-18.

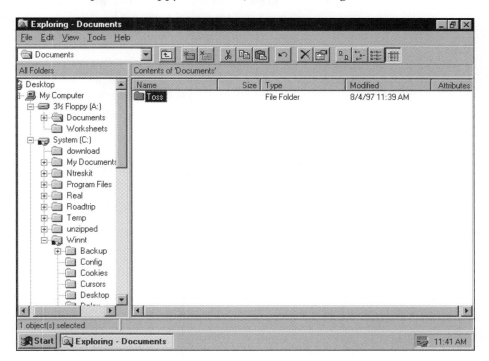

FIGURE 4-18

New folder in the Exploring window

MANIPULATING FOLDERS

After creating folders, you can move them, copy them, delete them, or rename them. Folder manipulation commands affect not only the folder itself, but also all the files and subfolders it contains.

MOVING FOLDERS

move An operation in which a selected object is removed from its original location and placed elsewhere.

When you **move** a folder, Windows NT places the folder and all its contents in the new location you indicate and then deletes the folder and any contents from its original location. In the following steps, you will learn to drag a folder from one location to another.

HANDS ON

1. Make sure your floppy disk is still in drive A: (or drive B:), and that the Exploring window is open and active on the Desktop with its toolbar displayed.

2. Select the **Documents** folder on the floppy disk.

3. Point to the **Toss** folder icon in the Contents pane.

4. With the left mouse button, drag the **Toss** folder to the **Worksheets** folder icon in the All Folders pane. When the **Worksheets** folder highlights, release the mouse button.

The Toss folder moves from its original location (the Documents folder) to the Worksheets folder. Notice that the Contents pane is now blank.

5. Select the **Worksheets** folder icon in the All Folders pane.

The folder opens, and its contents appear in the Contents pane. Notice that this folder contains the folder you just moved from the Documents folder. You may also use the Cut and Paste commands to move a folder from one location to another.

It is easy to "drop" an object into the wrong folder as you drag it across the Desktop. If that happens to you, click the toolbar's Undo button (identified on Figure 4-7) to return the dropped object to its original location so that you can start over.

COPYING FOLDERS

When you **copy** a folder, Windows NT duplicates that folder and its contents to the location you indicate; the original folder and contents remain where they were. In the following steps, you will copy a folder from one location to another.

HANDS ON

1. Point to the **Toss** folder.

2. Click and hold the right mouse button.

3. Drag the folder to the **Documents** folder in the All Folders pane.

4. Release the right mouse button.

A shortcut menu appears with options to move or copy the folder.

5. Click the Copy Here option.

Both the Worksheets and Documents folder have a Toss subfolder in them.

You may also use the Copy and Paste commands to copy a folder from one location to another.

copy (1) An operation which temporarily stores a duplicate of any selected object, such as text, image, file, or folder, in the computer's memory; (2) the name of the command that performs this operation; (3) any object that duplicates an original and, in the case of files or folders, may or may not have the same name as the original, depending on the copy's location.

DELETING FOLDERS

delete An operation which removes any selected item, such as text, image, file, or folder, from a disk; in Windows NT the deleted item is sent to the Recycle Bin, which holds it until it is either restored to its original location or removed permanently.

When you **delete** a folder from the C: drive, Windows NT removes it from its original location and places it in a holding area called the Recycle Bin, whose icon appears on your Desktop. From the Recycle Bin, you can remove objects permanently from storage or change your mind and restore them to their original locations. You'll learn more about the Recycle Bin in the next lesson.

Any object that you delete from a floppy disk is gone permanently. You should be sure you want to delete the folder or folders you intend to delete. It's not a good idea to delete folders that you have not created. They may be required by other users or by application software.

In the following steps, you will delete a folder.

HANDS ON

1. Click the **Documents** folder icon in the All Folders pane.

The folder opens and its contents appear in the Contents pane.

2. Click the **Toss** folder icon in the Contents pane.

The selected folder icon highlights.

3. Press Delete.

Since the Delete command permanently removes objects from storage, the Confirm Folder Delete dialog box appears asking "Are you sure you want to remove the folder 'Toss' and all its contents?"

4. Click Yes (or press Enter).

The selected folder is deleted from its parent folder, Documents.

RENAMING FOLDERS

rename To change the name of a file, a folder, or an icon.

When you **rename** a folder, you change its name. The File menu's Rename command allows you to change the name of any selected icon. Alternately, you can simply click an icon's name, wait while it highlights, and type the new name. In the following steps, you will use both of these techniques to change a folder's name.

HANDS ON

1. Click the **Worksheets** folder icon in the All Folders pane.

The folder opens and its contents appear in the Contents pane.

2. Click the **Toss** folder icon in the Contents pane.

The icon highlights.

3. Choose Rename from the File menu.

The highlighted folder's name appears in a text box with a blinking insertion point.

4. Type **Budgets-98** and press Enter.

The folder is renamed.

5. Point anywhere over the highlighted file name **Budgets-98** in the Contents pane, and click the file name again.

The highlighted folder's name appears in a text box with a blinking insertion point.

6. Type **Budgets-99** and press Enter.

7. If you want to quit your work, log off your computer. Otherwise, leave your computer in its current status, and complete the exercises that conclude this lesson.

LESSON SUMMARY AND EXERCISES

After you complete this lesson, you should know how to do the following:

USING THE WINDOWS NT EXPLORER

- Differentiate between the All Folders and Contents panes of the Exploring window.

CUSTOMIZING THE EXPLORING WINDOW

- Customize the Windows NT Explorer display to view disk contents in different ways.

- Expand the folder by clicking the (+) sign; collapse the folder by clicking the (−) sign.

WINDOW PANES

- Drag the border separating the two display panels to change their relative size.

FORMATTING DISKS

- Prepare a disk to hold data.

CREATING FOLDERS AND SUBFOLDERS

- Divide the disk into folders and subfolders for more efficient data storage. To create a main folder, select the drive and choose the New option from the File menu. To create a subfolder, highlight the folder to be the parent before using the New option.

MANIPULATING FOLDERS

- Move folders from one location to another by using either the drag-and-drop or cut-and-paste method.

- Copy an entire folder, including all of its files and subfolders with the drag-and-drop or copy-and-paste method.

- Change the name of a folder by using the Rename command.

- Remove a folder from disk with the Delete command.

NEW TERMS TO REMEMBER

After you complete this lesson, you should know the meaning of these terms:

application-
   oriented
   structure
copy
delete
Detail view
disk structure
file allocation table
   (FAT)
file system

formatting
main folder
move
NT file system
   (NTFS)
pane
parent folder
project-oriented
   structure
rename

root directory
separator line
status bar
Tool Tip
truncated
type
user-oriented
   structure
window pane

MATCHING EXERCISE

Match each of the terms with the definitions on the right:

TERMS	DEFINITIONS
1. copy	**a.** Process by which a new, blank disk is prepared properly for operation in a personal computer
2. delete	
3. pane	**b.** Lop off the end of an object's name when it is too long to be displayed
4. truncate	
5. format	**c.** A disk's top level folder, or root directory
6. main folder	**d.** A List or Detail view that displays objects sorted by file type and subsorted alphabetically
7. parent folder	
8. disk structure	**e.** Operation in which data stored in a file or folder is duplicated so that the original remains and the duplicate is stored in another disk location
9. status bar	
10. type	
	f. Remove an object from storage
	g. A window division
	h. The relationship of folders to subfolders
	i. A folder which contains other folders
	j. An area at the bottom of a window that explains selected objects or menu commands

COMPLETION EXERCISE

Fill in the missing word or phrase for each of the following:

1. The _____ _____ is the method used to control access to a disk.

2. To view the maximum number of objects in a window without scrolling, and still be able to drag them around the window, choose this view: _____.

3. The _____ in which folders on a disk are organized varies from system to system, depending on a user's preferences.

4. One way to move a file or folder from one disk location to another is to _____ the object's _____ .

5. The root of the entire Windows NT filing system is the _____ .

6. The _____ is a strip of tool buttons just below the menu bar.

7. To expand a collapsed folder in the Explorer's All Folders pane, press the _____ key.

8. The Exploring window's _____ pane displays the folders and files stored in the active or open folder.

9. The _____ view option displays the name, size, type, and date of each object in the Contents pane.

10. To _____ a file or folder, you select the file or folder and then type the new name.

SHORT-ANSWER QUESTIONS

Write a brief answer to each of the following questions:

1. Suppose your projects involve creating documents from a variety of data types—such as text, graphics, and numeric calculations. Which type of folder structure would likely work best for organizing your work? Why?

2. List and describe briefly what occurs when a blank disk is formatted.

3. What is the best thing to do with a disk that does not format properly?

4. You have seen several view options including large icon, small icon, list, and details. Differentiate among them, and explain when each view option might be useful.

5. Discuss briefly the various ways in which you can customize the Exploring window.

6. Compare and contrast the My Computer and Exploring windows. When might you use each?

7. What steps do you follow to move an object?

8. What steps do you follow to copy an object?

9. What steps do you follow to rename an object?

10. What steps do you follow to enlarge the Exploring window's Contents pane relative to its All Folders pane?

APPLICATION PROJECTS

Perform the following actions to complete these projects:

1. Format several blank disks, if possible, and save them for your future data storage needs. Be sure to select the proper disk capacity and type of format options.

2. Open your Exploring window and modify its appearance so that it looks similar to the Exploring window shown in Figure 4-19. Then make any adjustments you desire to customize its appearance to suit your needs.

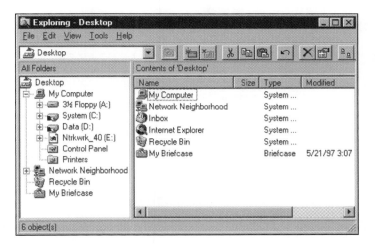

FIGURE 4-19

The customized Exploring window

3. Create a set of parent folders on a disk and then create some folders within them. Practice the various operations available for manipulating the folders: copy, move, rename, and delete. Practice using both the mouse and the appropriate Edit menu commands to accomplish the move and copy tasks.

4. On a blank, formatted disk, create an application-oriented folder structure that might be used by a small business. Begin by creating a set of new folders and label them accordingly. A small business might use a word processing application for letters and reports, a spreadsheet application to prepare budgets and cost analyses, and a database application to maintain a company's ledgers and payroll.

5. On the same disk you used for Application Project 4, create a user-oriented folder structure. You can set up the structure for yourself only or for several users. Create and name the folders accordingly. When you are finished working, log off.

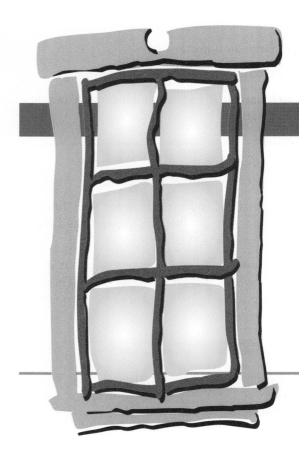

MANAGING
YOUR
FILES

OBJECTIVES

After you complete this lesson, you will be able to do the following:

- *Understand the necessity of managing disk storage.*

- *Recognize the names and types of files contained within folders.*

- *Recognize file types and their icons in the Explorer.*

- *Copy one or more files into a different folder or drive.*

- *Move files from one folder or drive to another.*

- *Delete files to remove them from a disk.*

- *Assign new names to files.*

- *Find files knowing only a portion of their names.*

- *Search for files by date, size, and location.*

CONTENTS

Managing Files

Creating Files

Working with File Types

Copying Files

Moving Files

Deleting Files

Restoring Deleted Files

Renaming Files

Searching for Files

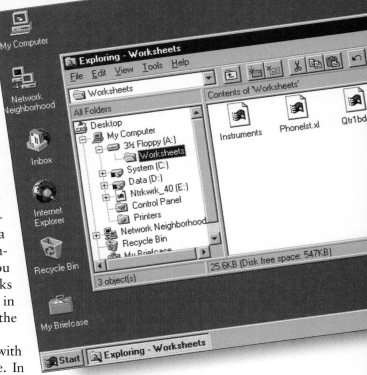

C reating, copying, moving, editing, and deleting files are all part of managing information so that you can work productively. Duplicating important files is essential to safe computing. Information stored in a single location may be accidentally deleted or destroyed. You can take these duplicate disks away from your computer in case something happens to the original files.

File organization begins with the creation of a disk structure. In the last lesson, you learned how to manipulate folders within a disk structure. Now you will learn how to create and manipulate files within those folders.

MANAGING FILES

file management The process of organizing and caring for your disks and files.

back up (v.) To copy (and/or compress) data for storage elsewhere in case it is needed to restore damaged or lost original data.

backup (n.) A copied and/or compressed set of data from which damaged or lost original data can be restored.

File management is the process of organizing and caring for your disks and files. It involves much more than just creating files or removing the ones you don't need. You may wish to share a letter or picture you create with a friend or colleague. When you know how to copy files, you can easily duplicate the contents of a file onto another disk or into another folder. Copying lets you **back up** or duplicate files onto floppy disks or other storage media.

Information stored in a single location may be accidentally deleted or destroyed. You can take these **backup** disks away from your computer in case something happens to the original files.

This lesson also shows you how to rename and move files on disk. You can accomplish all of these file management chores—delete, copy, rename, and move—with the keyboard or the mouse. You can manage files individually or in groups. Search methods help you locate files stored on your computer. You will master all of these techniques in the following exercises, using the Windows NT Explorer.

N O T E *Many of these exercises could also be done in the My Computer window, but the Exploring window is more convenient.*

CREATING FILES

Storing data properly means placing information on the correct disk drive so that it can be found later. To store information efficiently, in the form of files, you tell the operating system:

- On which drive to store the file
- In which folder to put the file
- By what name to identify the file
- By what type to create the file

FILE NAMES

file name The characters used to identify a file, limited to 255 characters in Windows 95 and Windows NT 4.0 and 8 characters in DOS and older versions of Windows.

extension A one- to three-character file name component that is used to identify the type of data stored in the file.

file-naming conventions The rules governing the length and character requirements for file names created within a specific operating system.

File names consist of two primary parts: the **file name**, which is a descriptive name that a user assigns to a data file, and an optional **extension** that follows the file name and specifies the type of data stored in the file. In the Windows NT 4.0 environment, file names follow two sets of rules.

MS-DOS FILE NAMES

Files created within the MS-DOS operating system, are named according to the following rules, known as **file-naming conventions**:

- The file name must contain at least one character but no more than eight characters.

- A period or "dot" separates the file name and its extension.

- The optional extension may have from one to three characters.

- Valid characters for the file name and extension are letters of the alphabet (A–Z), digits (0–9), and the following punctuation symbols:

$	Dollar sign	^	Circumflex or caret
_	Underscore	#	Pound sign
–	Hyphen	%	Percent sign
!	Exclamation point	&	Ampersand
{}	Braces	~	Tilde
()	Parentheses		

- Invalid characters include the following symbols:

	Space character	:	Colon
\	Backslash	+	Plus sign
/	Slash	=	Equal sign
<	Less-than sign	;	Semicolon
>	Greater-than sign	,	Comma
|	Pipe	?	Question mark
"	Quotation mark	*	Asterisk
[ ]	Square brackets	.	Period

- The extensions .EXE, .COM, .BAT, and .SYS are reserved for program files and files that contain instructions for operating system commands.

- File names can be entered with either uppercase or lowercase letters. Thus, LETTER1.DOC is the same file as Letter1.doc or letter1.doc; the MS-DOS operating system converts all file names to uppercase characters.

The limitations on the length of and type of characters in file names forced users to be creative when naming files. A memo written to J. Smith concerning a billing error, for instance, might be stored in a file named SMITHERR.MEM.

WINDOWS NT FILE NAMES

The Windows NT operating system provides much more descriptive freedom. File names can be up to 255 characters long, with spaces, more than one period, and only nine prohibited characters:

\	Backslash	|	Pipe
/	Slash	"	Quotation mark
:	Colon	*	Asterisk
<	Less-than sign	?	Question mark
>	Greater-than sign		

File extensions are still used, but they are not always displayed. Rather, they are automatically assigned by the software that creates the file.

While Windows NT supports both old and new file naming standards, not all versions of application software support both. Therefore, you must follow the old rules for MS-DOS file names when you are working with applications developed and released before the release of the Windows 95 and Windows NT operating systems—or if you share files with someone whose system uses MS-DOS.

MAKING A FILE

Remember that the three basic kinds of files are system files, program files, and document files. Unless you are a programmer, the files that you create are document files, the work that you do using a particular program.

Desktop accessory A small program built into the Windows NT operating system.

The Notepad is a **Desktop accessory**, a small program built in to Windows NT. The Notepad allows you to create or view short, unformatted text documents. These steps show you how to create a Notepad file and save it to the floppy disk you used in the last lesson. Begin by logging on to Windows NT and inserting your floppy disk into the appropriate drive.

HANDS ON

1. Use the Start menu (Programs then Accessories) to open the Notepad program. Figure 5-1 shows the way.

The Notepad program opens to display a window like the one shown in Figure 5-2.

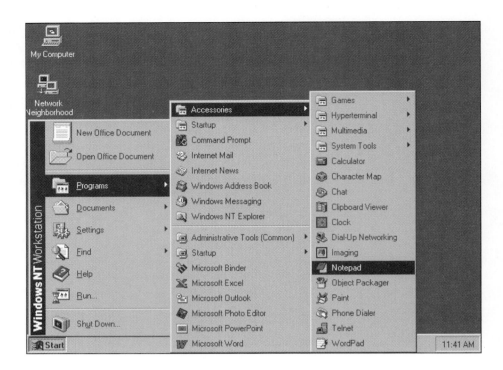

FIGURE 5-1

The Start menu

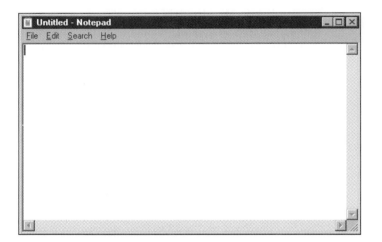

FIGURE 5-2

The Notepad window with an unsaved document

The window's title bar says "Untitled - Notepad." The word "untitled" indicates that the document in this window is unsaved; the document exists in the computer's memory but its file has not been stored.

The insertion point (blinking vertical line) in the document window shows where the next text you type will appear.

2. Type a few sentences.

The text you type appears in the Notepad document window.

3. Choose Save As from the File menu.

The Save As dialog box appears. The Save As dialog box lets you give Windows NT the information it needs to save your file: the file's location and its name. Figure 5-3 identifies the dialog box areas in which you provide this information.

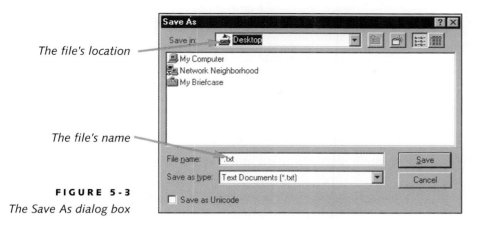

The file's location

The file's name

FIGURE 5-3
The Save As dialog box

4. Click the arrow to the right of the Save In text box.

A list of the storage devices attached to your computer drops down. The Save In box allows you to set the file's drive location.

5. Click the icon of the floppy drive that holds your disk (either A: or B:).

NOTE *Use the disk you formatted in Lesson 4 with the label Untitled.*

The drive location appears in the Save In text box. The Documents folder and others that you might have created, appear in the contents box immediately below.

6. Double-click the **Documents** folder.

The Documents folder appears in the Save In text box.

If you were to save the file now, Windows NT would place it in the Documents folder of your floppy disk.

7. Click the arrow to the right of the Save In text box.

A menu such as the one in Figure 5-4 drops down. This menu shows the file organization of the selected Save In location.

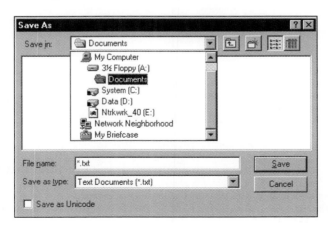

FIGURE 5-4
The Save In menu

8. Click outside the menu to close it without making a choice.

9. Press Tab twice—once to move to the Contents box and once to move to the File Name box.

The text in the File Name box highlights, ready for you to enter a new name.

HINT *Press Tab to move from one option box to another in nearly every dialog box in Windows NT.*

10. Type **MyNote**

MyNote replaces Untitled in the File Name box.

HINT *In spite of Windows NT's ability to use more flexible file names, you may want to use MS-DOS file names if you use your files on older computers.*

11. Click the Save button.

Windows NT writes the MyNote document into the Documents folder of your floppy disk. The dialog box closes, and the Notepad title bar changes to say "MyNote.txt-Notepad."

12. Close the Notepad window.

13. Open the Windows NT Explorer and select the **Documents** folder in your floppy disk.

14. Choose Details from the View menu.

Your Exploring window should resemble Figure 5-5. The All Folders pane shows the organization of your disk with the addition of your saved file. The Contents pane shows your file's name, size, type, and modification date.

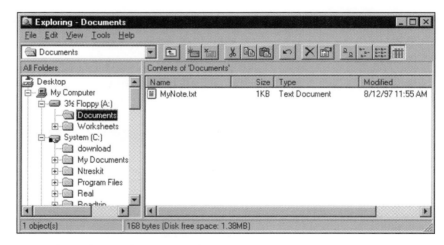

FIGURE 5-5
The Exploring window

15. Close the Exploring window.

16. Remove your floppy disk from the disk drive.

WORKING WITH FILE TYPES

Figure 5-4 shows a Save As dialog box option that you did not change: Save As Type. File type is a functional category—such as text document file, bitmapped image document application file, or system file. Every file on your system has a file type. Windows NT recognizes dozens of file types when first installed. As application software is added to the system, additional file types are created.

WARNING   *The three character file extension identifies the file type. Do not assign your own extensions to files if you want Windows NT to recognize the program that created the file.*

VIEWING FILE TYPES

In this activity, you will examine the types of files on your Student Data Disk.

HANDS ON

1. Insert your Student Data Disk.

2. Open the Windows NT Explorer and maximize its window.

3. In the All Folders pane, click the icon of your floppy drive to display its contents in the Contents pane.

4. Check that Details are displayed in the Contents window. If not, choose Details from the View menu.

5. Drag to enlarge the Details headings until you can see all the information in each Details column.

6. Click the Type heading.

COPYING FILES

Now the Contents window is organized by Type. It contains 6 different kinds of objects. The same techniques that you used to move or copy folders in Lesson 4 apply to moving or copying files:

- Dragging a file or folder from one disk to another disk copies that object.

- Dragging a file or folder from one folder to another folder on the same disk moves that object.

- Using the right button to drag a file or folder from one folder to another folder on the same disk copies that object.

COPYING INTO THE SAME FOLDER

Because no two files in the same folder can have the same file name, you must rename the copy if you want to place a copy in the original folder.

If you drag a file into a folder that already contains an identically named file, the Confirm File Replace dialog box, as shown in Figure 5-6, appears. The sizes and creation dates of the files are displayed in the dialog box to help you decide whether to replace the file. If you click Yes, the existing file is erased and replaced with the one you dragged and dropped.

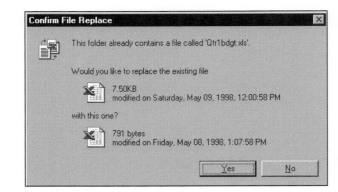

FIGURE 5-6
*The Confirm File
Replace
dialog box*

COPYING A FILE

In the following steps, you will copy a file from your Student Data Disk to your computer's hard disk.

HANDS ON

1. Select the **ShopList.txt** file in the Contents pane.

The file highlights.

2. Drag the **ShopList.txt** file onto the C: drive in the All Files pane, but do not release the mouse.

The pointer becomes an Object Copy pointer, as shown in Figure 5-7. It is ready to copy the selected file.

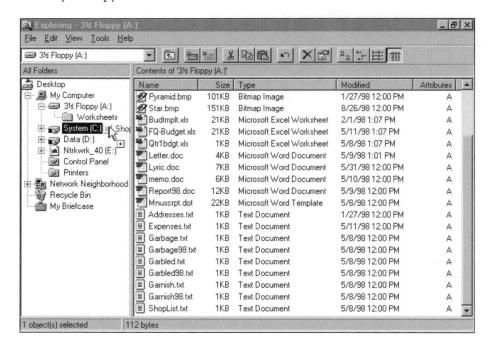

FIGURE 5-7
The Object Copy pointer

3. Release the mouse button.

The ShopList.txt file copies to the main folder of the hard disk.

4. Click the C: drive and locate the copied file.

Notice that it is named ShopList.txt just like the original.

NOTE   *You may have to scroll the Contents pane to see the file.*

COPYING ANOTHER FILE

In the following steps, you will copy the original file to another disk.

HANDS ON

1. Remove your Student Data Disk from the floppy drive, and insert the blank disk you used earlier in this lesson (and formatted in Lesson 4).

2. Collapse the C: drive so that you can see icons of all your devices in the All Folders pane if necessary.

3. Select the C: drive, if it is not already selected.

Its contents appear in the Contents pane.

4. Change the Contents view to List so that you can see as many objects as possible in its pane.

5. Locate the **ShopList.txt** file in the Contents pane. Scroll if necessary.

6. Drag **ShopList.txt** to the device icon in the All Folders pane for the drive that contains the floppy disk (A: or B:), and release the mouse button when the device icon highlights.

The file copies from the hard disk drive (C:) to the disk in drive A: (or B:).

7. Select the device icon for the drive that contains the disk (drive A: or B:).

The file name for the copied file appears in the Contents pane.

TIP   *You know two ways to copy folders and files—right-click dragging and holding* Ctrl *while dragging with the left button. Right-click dragging is safer, since you can confirm your intentions after you drag on the shortcut menu. If you use* Ctrl *and the left button, be sure to release the button before you release* Ctrl*. Otherwise, you will move a file—not copy the file.*

SELECTING MULTIPLE OBJECTS

Often it is convenient to manipulate a group of files together. When you want to copy, move, or otherwise handle several files, you select them as a group, and then manipulate them all together. The following mouse and keyboard techniques let you select more than one file at a time:

- To select files listed consecutively, click the first file, hold down Shift, and then click the last file in the list. All of the files between the first and last files are selected.

- To select noncontiguous files, click the first file, hold down Ctrl, and then click each of the files you want. Only the files you click are selected.

COPYING MULTIPLE FILES

In the following steps, you will select and copy a group of files.

HANDS ON

1. Begin with your Student Data Disk in drive A: (or B:) and the Exploring window open and maximized.

2. Select the device icon in the All Folders pane for the drive that contains your Student Data Disk (A: or B:).

3. Click the Details icon.

4. Click the file name **Letter.doc**.

5. Point to the file name **Mnuscrpt.dot**.

6. Press and hold (Shift), click the file name **Mnuscrpt.dot**, and then release (Shift) (and the mouse button).

All consecutively listed files from **Letter** through **Mnuscrpt** are selected, as shown in Figure 5-8.

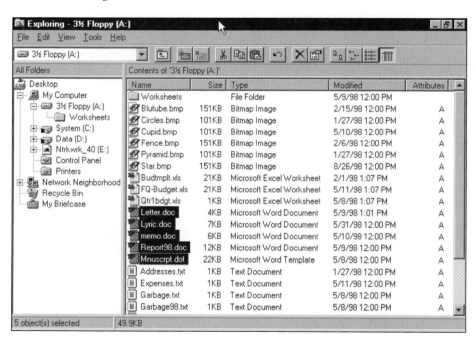

FIGURE 5-8

Five consecutive highlighted files

7. Point to any of the selected files.

8. Press (Ctrl) and drag the group of selected files to the **Worksheets** folder icon in the Contents pane.

9. Release the mouse button; then release (Ctrl).

The Copying dialog box appears as the selected files copy to the **Worksheets** folder on the Student Data Disk. Each copy will have the same name as the original file on the Student Data Disk's main folder.

NOTE   *If you did not see the Copying dialog box, you probably forgot to hold down the (Ctrl) key as you dragged. Choose Undo Move from the Edit menu and try again.*

10. Double-click the **Worksheets** folder in the Contents pane.

The Contents pane displays the copied file names.

MOVING FILES

Sometimes you will want to move a file from one folder to another. For example, when you have a folder for current projects and another for recently completed projects, you may want to move files you have finished working with into the "completed" folder. You may also want to move files that you rarely use to a floppy disk so they don't occupy valuable hard disk space.

The methods used to move files are similar to those you learned when copying files. If you are dragging between folders on the same disk, you do not hold down Ctrl.

In this exercise, you will practice moving files.

HANDS ON

1. Begin with your Student Data Disk in drive A: (or B:), the Exploring window open and maximized, and the **Worksheets** folder selected.

2. Display the toolbar if necessary. (Choose Toolbar from the View menu.)

3. Expand the floppy drive, if necessary, and examine its hierarchy.

The floppy disk has two levels, the main folder level and the **Worksheets** folder level. The Worksheets level should be currently selected.

4. Click the Up One Level button on the toolbar.

The main folder level is now selected. The Contents pane displays the contents of the Student Data Disk's main folder.

5. Drag the **Addresses.txt** file into the **Worksheets** folder.

The selected file moves into the **Worksheets** folder on your Student Data Disk.

6. Select the **Worksheets** folder in the All Folders pane.

Notice that the Contents pane displays the **Addresses** file.

7. Click the Up One Level button on the toolbar.

Notice that the file name **Addresses** no longer appears in the Student Data Disk's main folder.

MOVING A FILE OUTSIDE A FOLDER

In the following steps, you will move a file outside the folders on a disk.

HANDS ON

1. Select the **Worksheets** folder icon in the All Folders pane.

The contents of the selected folder appear in the Contents pane.

2. Point to the **Addresses** file.

3. Drag the file onto the icon for the drive that contains your Student Data Disk (drive A: or B:) in the All Folders pane. Release the mouse button when the drive icon highlights.

The file is moved from the **Worksheets** folder on your Student Data Disk to its main folder.

4. Select the icon for the drive that contains your Student Data Disk.

The contents of the disk's main folder appear in the Contents pane. Notice that the file you moved appears in the list.

MOVING A FILE BETWEEN DISKS

In the following steps, you will practice moving a file from one disk drive to another, using the drag-and-drop method.

HANDS ON

1. Expand the floppy drive icon that contains your Student Data Disk icon in the All Folders pane, if necessary.

The **Worksheets** folder on the Student Data Disk appears in the All Folders pane.

2. Select the device icon for disk drive C:.

The contents of the hard disk's (drive C:) main folder appear in the Contents pane.

3. Scroll the list in the Contents pane until the file name **ShopList.txt** becomes visible.

4. Select (highlight) the file name **ShopList.txt**.

5. Point to the selected file.

6. Press and hold the *right* mouse button, drag the selected file to the **Worksheets** folder icon (below the device icon for the drive that contains your Student Data Disk), and release the mouse button when the folder icon highlights.

A pop-up menu appears.

7. Select Move Here.

The selected file is moved from the main folder on the hard disk drive (C:) to the **Worksheets** folder on your Student Data Disk in drive A: (or B:).

DELETING FILES

Files that you no longer need can quickly fill up even the largest hard disk drive, so it is often necessary to delete files from time to time. Deleting a file removes the data from the disk. That's not an action to be taken lightly. If you find that you have accidentally deleted a file you need, you may be able to recover it if you act soon. You will learn about how to restore deleted files later in this lesson.

It is relatively safe to delete a file you named and created, after it has served its purpose. However, files placed on the hard drive during the installation of software are often critical to the operation of the software. A good rule to follow is not to remove any files in a program folder whose name or function you do not recognize. In order to remove the program itself, use either the program's uninstall feature (if available) or the Add/Remove Programs program in the Windows NT Control Panel folder.

WARNING   *Before deleting a program, scan through its folder to make sure you have no personal work stored there.*

When you want to delete a file from a folder, select the file and press Delete. A warning box appears as shown in Figure 5-9, forcing you to confirm your intentions before the file is removed from the disk.

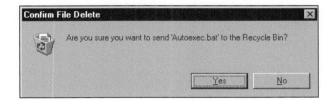

FIGURE 5-9
*Confirm File Delete
dialog box*

TIP   *Use Select All in the Edit menu to select all of the files in the active folder. The Invert Selection option deselects any files you have selected and selects all of the others; that is, it reverses the highlighting in the Contents area.*

DELETING MULTIPLE FILES

In the following steps, you will select multiple files that are not listed consecutively in the Contents pane and delete them.

HANDS ON

1. Select the device icon for the drive that contains your Student Data Disk (drive A: or B:).

2. Select the file name **ShopList.txt**.

3. While pressing Ctrl, select the file name **Budtmplt.xls**, then release Ctrl.

    The two files—**ShopList.txt** and **Budtmplt.xls**—are selected.

4. Press Delete.

    The Confirm Multiple File Delete dialog box appears on the Desktop. It asks you if you are sure you want to delete these two items.

5. Click Yes.

    The selected files are deleted from your floppy disk.

RESTORING DELETED FILES

Files that are deleted from a floppy disk are immediately removed from storage. When you delete a file from a hard disk, however, it is not removed from the disk immediately. Instead, its icon is placed in the Recycle Bin but the file itself remains in storage.

The Desktop's Recycle Bin icon resembles a wastebasket. When the Recycle Bin is empty, the wastebasket appears empty. When you delete items to the Recycle Bin, however, its icon appears to be full of pieces of paper. (This tells you the Recycle Bin is not empty!) To restore an item from the Recycle Bin, you open it to a window (shown in Figure 5-10), click the item, and choose Undo Delete from the Edit menu.

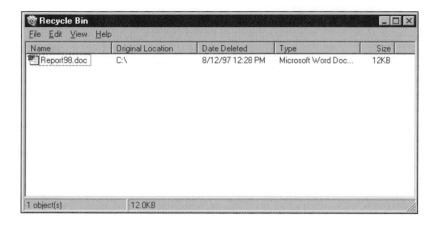

Name	Original Location	Date Deleted	Type	Size
Report98.doc	C:\	8/12/97 12:28 PM	Microsoft Word Doc...	12KB

1 object(s)   12.0KB

FIGURE 5-10

The Recycle Bin window

To permanently clear all the contents of the Recycle Bin, choose the Empty Recycle Bin command on the File menu. Check your Recycle Bin's contents periodically, especially any time you discover that your available hard disk space is getting low. Files you have deleted occupy disk space while they are stored in the Recycle Bin, so removing them from the Recycle Bin will free up hard disk space.

TIP   *Right-click on the Deskop's Recycle Bin icon to empty it. Double-click to open the Desktop's Recycle Bin.*

RESTORING A DELETED FILE

In the following steps, you will copy a file to the C: drive, delete it, and restore it.

HANDS ON

1. Make sure your Student Data Disk is inserted properly in drive A: (or drive B:).

2. Copy the **Pyramid.bmp** file from your Student Data Disk to C:.

3. Click C: in the All Folders pane and locate **Pyramid.bmp** in the Contents pane.

4. Click **Pyramid.bmp** in the Contents pane and press (Delete).

The Confirm File Delete dialog box appears asking "Are you sure you want to send "Pyramid.bmp" to the Recycle Bin?"

5. Click Yes.

6. Scroll the All Folders pane, if necessary, so that you can see the Recycle Bin system icon.

7. Click the Recycle Bin icon.

The Recycle Bin's contents appears in the Contents pane. Notice that it contains **Pyramid.bmp**.

N O T E   *You might see some additional files in the Recycle Bin window.*

8. Click the file **Pyramid.bmp** to highlight it.

9. Choose Restore from the File menu.

Pyramid.bmp returns to its location on the C: disk drive.

10. Repeat steps 3-5.

The file is no longer on the C: drive.

ENAMING FILES

Changing the name of a file is simple. You do this with the Rename command, or you can change the file's name directly in the Exploring window. As with deleting and removing files, you must use caution. You should only rename those files you created, since program files have specific meaning to the software that uses them.

Renaming a file involves two separate, single-click mouse actions. First, you select the file whose name you wish to change. Then you click the file name again. When you do this, the highlighted file name appears in a text box along with a blinking vertical line. This line is called the **insertion point**. If you now type a new file name, the new name completely replaces the old name. Alternatively, you can press → or ← to move the insertion point to a specific character in the file name and make minor changes to it without replacing the entire name. Table 5-1 lists the keystrokes you can use to move the insertion point for editing (renaming) a file name.

insertion point A small blinking vertical line that indicates where the next character typed at the keyboard will appear on screen.

TABLE 5-1:   USING THE INSERTION POINT

KEY	PURPOSE
←	Moves the insertion point one space to the left
→	Moves the insertion point one space to the right
Home	Moves the insertion point to the left of the first character
End	Moves the insertion point to the right of the last character
Ctrl + ←	Moves the insertion point to the beginning of the previous word
Ctrl + →	Moves the insertion point to the beginning of the next word
Delete	Removes the character to the right of the insertion point
Backspace	Removes the character to the left of the insertion point
Ctrl + Delete	Removes all characters to the right of the insertion point

RENAMING A FILE IN THE EXPLORING WINDOW

In the following steps, you will select and rename a file.

HANDS ON

1. Make sure the Contents pane displays the contents of the main folder of your Student Data Disk.

2. Click the file name **Circles.bmp** and wait until it highlights.

3. Click the highlighted file name **Circles.bmp** a second time.

A box surrounds the file name, which appears highlighted, as shown in Figure 5-11. Notice that a blinking insertion point appears at the end of the file's name.

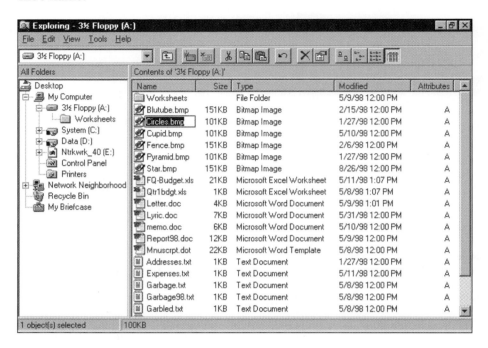

FIGURE 5-11
The highlighted file name

WARNING   *Click, wait, click is not the same command sequence as a double-click. If you double-click Circles, the Paint desk accessory and the Circles document file will open. Choose Exit from the File menu to close both the document and the application that created it.*

4. Type **Color Rings.bmp** and press (Enter).

The file name is changed. Notice that it remains selected.

WARNING   *If file extensions are not hidden in the Options View dialog box, you must enter the extension when you rename a file. If the extensions are hidden, Windows NT will add the extension automatically.*

RENAMING A FILE WITH THE RENAME COMMAND

Some people prefer the Rename command to worrying about accidentally double-clicking and opening an application. In the following steps, you will use the File menu's Rename command to change a file name.

**HANDS
ON**

1. Select the file name **Lyric.doc**.

2. Select the File menu in the Exploring window.

3. Select Rename.

A box surrounds the highlighted file name.

4. Type **Poem.doc** and press ⎡Enter⎤.

The file name is changed.

SEARCHING FOR FILES

Find An operation that attempts to locate: (1) a folder or file by identifying its network, disk drive, or folder; (2) specific content within a document by selecting and displaying it.

Disk drives may contain thousands of files in dozens of folders. Finding a file can be a tedious process if you cannot remember the name of the file or the folder in which it is located. Fortunately, the Explorer has a function that searches for files. The more you know about the name, folder, or date of a file, the easier it is to locate. Even if you know none of this information, you can locate a file if you can specify some of the text it contains.

The **Find** option is in the Tools menu. You will use the Files or Folders option in this lesson to locate files on your personal computer system.

SEARCHING: NAME AND LOCATION

The Find window has three tabs: Name & Location, Date Modified, and Advanced. The Name & Location tab initiates a search once you enter the name of the file, the drive in which to search, and the level of folders to be searched. If you want to search all disk drives, change the Look In text box to My Computer, as shown in Figure 5-12. To limit the search to the drive's main folder, make sure the Include Subfolders check box is *not* checked. To look in particular folders, enter the folder name in the Look In text box or click the Browse button. Here you are able to select the particular folder or folders you want to search.

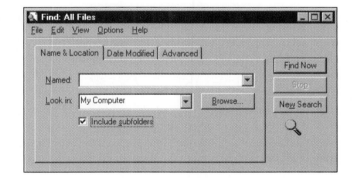

FIGURE 5-12

The Name & Location tab of the Find: All Files dialog box

If you know the name of the file you are trying to locate, type the file name in the Named text box.

USING WILDCARD CHARACTERS

wildcard character Character that you can use in a Find operation to represent either a single unknown character or multiple consecutive characters (called strings).

Wildcard characters are keyboard placeholder characters that you use when searching to represent unknown characters. If you are trying to locate a file, for example, but know only part of its name, you can type wildcard characters to stand for characters you're not sure of. Windows NT uses two wildcard characters: asterisk or star (*) and question mark (?). The asterisk represents any string of consecutive characters, including a single character. For example, searching for Letter* in the Named text box would find any and all files that begin with *Letter*. This includes Letter1, Letter August 96, Letter Smith, Letterman, and so on. If you know the beginning of a file name, you can search for it by typing as many characters as you know, followed by an asterisk.

The question mark wildcard represents any single character in the position in which it is typed. Use the question mark when you are uncertain about characters at the beginning or middle of the file name. For example, if you are looking for a document that starts with three characters you are not sure of, enter ??? followed by the characters you are sure of. For example, searching for ???Memo would find, OctMemo, JoeMemo, or 101Memo, but not OctoberMemo or Joseph Memo.

FINDING FILES BY NAME AND LOCATION

In the following steps, you will practice finding files using wildcard characters.

HANDS ON

1. Make sure the Contents pane displays the contents of the main folder on your Student Data Disk.

2. Choose Find from the Tools menu.

   The Find menu pops up.

3. Click Files or Folders.

   The Find: All Files dialog box appears, as shown in Figure 5-12.

4. Type **gar*** in the Named text box.

5. Click the Look In arrow to display its drop-down list of device icons.

6. Click the device icon for the drive that contains your Student Data Disk (drive A: or B:).

7. Click the Find Now button.

   Windows NT Explorer searches for all file names in the selected location that begin with the characters *gar*. When it finds the file or files that match the criteria, the bottom of the dialog box expands to list the files found.

8. Click the New Search button.

   The message box shown in Figure 5-13 appears warning you that the current search will be cleared.

9. Click OK.

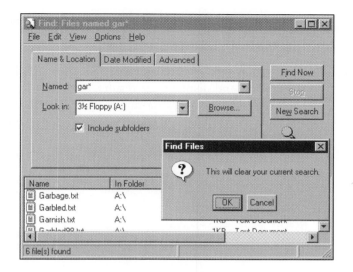

FIGURE 5-13

The Find Files warning box

SEARCHING SUBFOLDERS OR ONLY IN THE MAIN FOLDER

In the following steps, you will use the question mark wildcard character to find a specific file.

HANDS ON

1. Make sure the Find dialog box is active on the Desktop.

2. Type **Report??** in the Named text box.

3. Click the Look In arrow.

4. Click the device icon for the drive that contains your Student Data Disk (drive A: or B:).

5. Make sure the Include Subfolders box is *not* checked.

6. Click Find Now.

Windows NT searches for all file names in the selected location that begin with the letters *Report* and that end with any two characters. When it finds any files that match the criteria, Find expands the bottom of its dialog box to list the one criteria-matching file found in the specified location (the main folder of drive A: or B:).

Figure 5-14 shows the search results, one file found.

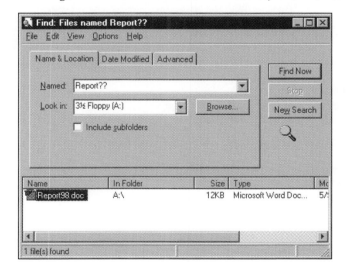

FIGURE 5-14

Search results, Report??
without Subfolders

7. Click the Include Subfolders check box to add the check mark.

8. Click Find Now.

Windows NT searches for all file names in the selected location that meet the criteria and displays the results, as shown in Figure 5-15. Notice that this time Find lists two criteria-matching files found in the specified location (the root directory on drive A: or B: and the folder stored in the disk's main folder).

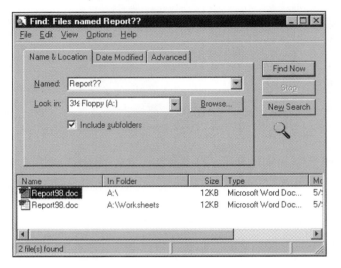

FIGURE 5-15

Search results, Report??
including Subfolders

9. Click New Search and then OK to clear the dialog box.

SEARCHING: DATE MODIFIED

Even if you remember nothing of the name, location, or contents of a file, the Explorer can find the file if you remember when you created or last modified the file. The Date Modified tab presents a window, as shown in Figure 5-16. The default is to find all files as indicated by the first button. The Find All Files Created Or Modified option has three subchoices so that you can enter a range of dates to be searched or specify how many days or months back from today you want to search.

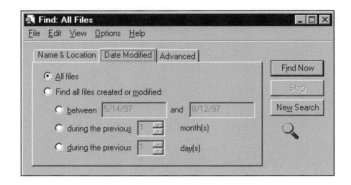

FIGURE 5-16

The Date Modified tab of
the Find: All Files
dialog box

SEARCHING: ADVANCED

The Advanced tab of the Find: All Files dialog box is shown in Figure 5-17. The Of Type box lets you search for files of a particular type, such as Microsoft Word documents. The Containing Text box lets you enter words or phrases that you know are in the file, such as an unusual last name for someone you wrote a letter to. Finally, the Size Is text box lets you specify an upper or lower limit to the size of the file, in kilobytes.

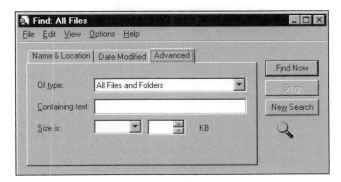

FIGURE 5-17

The Advanced Tab of the Find: All Files dialog box

FINDING FILES BY DATE

In the following steps, you will find files that were modified during specific dates.

HANDS ON

1. Make sure the Contents pane displays the contents of the main folder on your Student Data Disk.

2. If the Find dialog box is not open, choose Find from the Tools menu, and select Files or Folders.

3. If necessary, select the device icon for the drive that contains your Student Data Disk (drive A: or B:) from the Look In drop-down list.

4. Click the Date Modified tab.

5. Click the Between radio button.

   The two Date text boxes become active.

6. Double-click the first (left) text box (or press Tab).

   The date highlights for easy replacement.

7. Type **1/25/98** and press Tab.

   The second text box (right) highlights.

8. Type **1/28/98**.

9. Press Enter.

   Windows NT searches your Student Data Disk and locates and lists those files that were modified between the specified dates.

10. Close the Find dialog box.

    The Find dialog box is removed from the Desktop.

11. If you want to quit your work on the computer, log off your system. Otherwise, leave your computer in its current status and complete the exercises for this lesson.

LESSON SUMMARY AND EXERCISES

After you complete this lesson, you should know how to do the following:

MANAGING FILES

■ Explain the purpose of creating, copying, moving, and deleting files.

■ Explain the importance of having backup copies of your files.

CREATING FILES

■ Use the Save As dialog box to set a file's drive, folder, name, and type.

■ Understand the Windows NT and MS-DOS rules for naming files.

WORKING WITH FILE TYPES

■ Use the Windows NT Explorer to identify an object's file type.

COPYING FILES

■ Drag to move a file from one folder to another on the same disk or to copy a file from one folder to another on different disks.

■ Hold down Ctrl and drag to copy a file from one folder to another on the same disk.

■ Select consecutive files by clicking the first file in the Contents panel, holding down Shift, and clicking the last file.

■ Select non-consecutive files by clicking the first file, holding down Ctrl, and clicking each file you want to select.

MOVING FILES

■ Click the Up One Level button, then drag the file to its new location to move it to a new folder on the same disk.

■ Select the file and drag onto the drive icon to move a file outside a folder.

■ Select the file using the right mouse button, then drag the file icon into the folder on the new disk to move a file to a different disk.

DELETING FILES

■ Understand the risks of deleting files.

■ Click the file to be removed and press Delete. To confirm the deletion, click Yes in the Confirm File Delete dialog box.

RESTORING DELETED FILES

■ Double-click the Recycle Bin Desktop icon. Select the files to be undeleted, and click the Restore option of the File menu.

RENAMING FILES

■ Select the file to be renamed. Click the file name to highlight it. Type a new name or edit the name that appears in the box beside the file type icon.

SEARCHING FOR FILES

■ Use the Find, Files or Folders command on the Tools menu.

■ Click the Date Modified tab of the Find: All Files window to limit the search within particular dates.

NEW TERMS TO REMEMBER

After you complete this lesson, you should know the meaning of these terms:

back up	file management	Find
backup	file name	insertion point
Desktop accessory	file-naming	wildcard character
extension	conventions	

MATCHING EXERCISE

Match each of the terms with the definitions on the right:

TERMS	DEFINITIONS
1. back up	**a.** Procedure for changing the name of a file
2. copy	**b.** Procedure by which folders on a disk are searched to locate one or more files based on user-supplied criteria
3. delete	
4. Find	**c.** Symbol or character that is used to represent either a single character or a string of consecutive characters
5. insertion point	
6. move	**d.** Procedure for creating a duplicate set of data that can be used if the original data is ever destroyed
7. rename	
8. wildcard character	**e.** Procedure for removing entirely a set of data from a disk
9. extension	
10. file name	**f.** Procedure for creating an exact duplicate of data stored in a file and placing it in another disk location with either the same name as the original file or a different name
	g. Under old DOS rules, a part of a file name that is from one to eight characters and that tells the user the contents of the file
	h. Procedure for removing data from its original disk location to another disk location
	i. A three-character part of a file name that identifies the type of data stored in the file
	j. Blinking line in a text or an edit box that can be positioned to insert, delete, or type characters

COMPLETION EXERCISE

Fill in the missing word or phrase for each of the following:

1. A small program built into Windows NT is known as a(n) _____.

2. One way that Windows NT allows you to copy or move a file is by _____ the file to another disk or directory.

3. You can _____ a file to remove it from a disk.

4. When you _____ a file, its name is changed but its data remains unaltered.

5. Clicking a selected file name or folder name causes a(n) _____ to appear, which allows you to edit the file or folder name.

6. When you _____ data by copying it to another disk, you are safeguarding it in case you lose the original data.

7. Windows NT allows you to _____ a file based on its name, location, or the date it was last modified.

8. The _____ is a wildcard character that represents a string of consecutive characters.

9. The _____ is a wildcard character that represents a single character.

10. The Windows NT operating system now makes it possible for users to create _____ that are up to 255 characters.

SHORT-ANSWER QUESTIONS

Write a brief answer to each of the following questions:

1. What is the name of the Windows NT program that you use primarily for managing data stored on disks?

2. Why is the Copy operation the most commonly used file management procedure?

3. Describe the two methods that Windows NT provides for moving a file or folder from one disk location to another.

4. List the precautions you should take before deleting a file.

5. Suppose you cannot remember the name of a file with which you last worked one week ago, or which folder it is in. Describe how you might go about locating the file.

6. What information does the operating system need in order to save a file?

7. What characters are prohibited in a Windows NT file name?

8. What happens if you drag a file into a folder that already has the same file name?

9. How do you select a group of contiguous objects in a list window? A group of non-contiguous objects?

10. What steps should you follow if the object that you are trying to rename accidentally opens? Why does this sometimes happen?

APPLICATION PROJECTS

Insert your Student Data Disk into drive A: (or drive B:). Perform the following actions to complete these projects:

1. Use the Exploring window to create four new folders on your Student Data Disk. Label them **WP-Files, Spreadsheets, DB-Files,** and **Graphics,** respectively. Click the Details button, if necessary, to view a detailed list of your Student Data Disk. Copy the **Letter, Memo,** and **Mnuscrpt** files to the **WP-Files** folder. Move the **Color Rings, Fence,** and **Pyramid** files to the **Graphics** folder. Move the **Addresses** file to the **DB-Files** folder.

2. Open the Exploring window, if necessary. Open the **WP-Files** folder and create a folder labeled **Memos** inside it. Move all of the **Garbage, Garbled,** and **Garnish** files inside the **Memos** folder. Expand the disk icon to see its hierarchy in the All Folders pane.

3. Open the Notepad Desktop accessory. Write a memo to someone and save it as **My Memo.** When you save the file, set its location to the **Memos** folder you created in the last application project.

4. Open the Exploring window, if necessary. Open the **Worksheets** folder. Select the **Report98** file and rename it **Report99.** Move the file you just renamed to the **Memos** folder. Next, open the **Worksheets** folder. Select the **Instruments** file and rename it **Instrument List,** and then change the name of the **Phonelst** file to **Phone List.** Move the two files you've just renamed to the **DB-Files** folder.

5. Open the Exploring window, if necessary. Use the Find command on the Tools menu to locate all files on your Student Data Disk that end with **98.** Be sure to use the appropriate wildcard character or characters to conduct the search. How many files that end with **98** did you find? Now use the Find operation again to search for all files on your Student Data Disk that were modified after May 30, 1998. How many are there? When you are finished working, log off the computer.

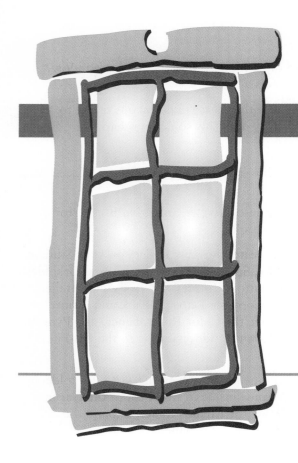

LESSON 6

WINDOWS NT
ACCESSORIES

OBJECTIVES

*After you complete this lesson, you will be able to do the
following:*

- *Identify the Accessory categories included in Windows NT.*

- *Use the Calculator to perform simple calculations.*

- *Create, save, open, edit, and set options for both text
and formatted documents with WordPad.*

- *Draw pictures using Paint.*

- *Recognize the communications accessories used to
send and receive data through a network, telephone,
computer, or fax.*

- *Use a browser to explore the World Wide Web.*

T he first personal computer operating systems met the basic requirements of booting the computer, managing system resources, managing file storage, and running application software. Users who had to type documents—simple or complex—purchased word processing programs. Spreadsheet and database management software, games, educational programs, and data communications all required separate purchases. If the program met a central need of the user, the expense ($100–$500) was cost-effective. For the person who typed one or two letters a month, however, the price of a full-featured word processor was too high.

Software manufacturers filled this gap by offering inexpensive software (often less than $100). As operating systems evolved, more of these features have been provided with the operating system. Lesson 6 introduces you to many of the small application programs that are included with Windows NT.

NTRODUCING WINDOWS NT ACCESSORIES

Windows calls these small application programs **accessories**. Several categories of accessories—also called **applets**—are available in Windows NT.

GENERAL-PURPOSE ACCESSORIES

Applets in this category range from serious (a small word processor) to not so serious (a drawing program) to recreational (games). Table 6-1 lists some of these programs and their functions.

accessories (or **applets**)
Operating system programs or third-party software that supplement Windows NT 4.0 with application features, such as editing, drawing, and communications.

TABLE 6-1: GENERAL-PURPOSE ACCESSORIES

NAME	FUNCTION
Briefcase	A file management tool for synchronizing the files stored on different computers. You can connect the computers with cables or use floppy disks or telephone connections to synchronize files when the computers are in different locations.
Calculator	An on-screen calculator used both for simple arithmetic and more complex scientific calculations.
Clipboard Viewer	A tool for viewing the current contents of the Windows Clipboard, a portion of RAM that holds data temporarily for later retrieval.
NotePad	A text editing program used to create and view short, unformatted text documents.

TABLE 6-1: GENERAL-PURPOSE ACCESSORIES, continued

NAME	FUNCTION
Paint	A painting program used to create and modify images in black-and-white or color.
WordPad	A word/text processing program that allows you to type formatted letters, memos, and other text documents. WordPad also lets you revise text files used by the operating system.
Screen Savers	A set of moving images that help prevent damage to the monitor's screen when the computer has been idle for a long time.

COMMUNICATIONS ACCESSORIES

Windows NT includes several applets to assist you in sending and receiving digital information from one computer to another. To run some of these applications, you must have a modem installed on your computer. Table 6-2 summarizes these accessories.

TABLE 6-2: COMMUNICATIONS ACCESSORIES

NAME	FUNCTION
Dial-Up Networking	Allows your computer to connect to remote computer networks using your modem or cables.
HyperTerminal	Connects your computer to another computer, even if it isn't running Windows. Requires a modem.
Phone Dialer	Places telephone calls from your computer through a modem.
Windows Messaging	Handles the sending and receiving of electronic mail (e-mail). Mail can be exchanged with users on your network or outside your network via modem.
Chat	Lets you conduct a written "conversation" with another user on your network.
Telnet	Lets you log on to another computer network via modem. Telnet is both a program and a set of rules that sets up your computer as a terminal on the remote network.

MULTIMEDIA ACCESSORIES

multimedia Documents or software which combine sound, text, graphics, animation, and/or video.

Multimedia consists of sound, text, graphics, animation, and video combined into a single application software package. The accessories in this group let you control any multimedia hardware devices attached to your computer system, such as CD-ROM drives, speakers, video players, or sound cards. Table 6-3 briefly describes these applets.

TABLE 6-3: MULTIMEDIA ACCESSORIES

NAME	FUNCTION
CD Player	Plays audio compact disks from a CD-ROM drive connected to your computer.
Media Player	Plays audio and video clips. Controls multimedia hardware devices.

TABLE 6-3: MULTIMEDIA ACCESSORIES, continued

NAME	FUNCTION
Sound Recorder	Records, edits, and plays back sound files. Lets you insert sound files into documents.
Volume Control	Controls volume and balance of a sound card.

Reading about Windows NT accessories is like listening to someone talk about how to drive a car. The only way to really learn to drive is to get behind the wheel and do it. In the following section, you will learn the basic functions of several Windows NT accessories.

USING THE WINDOWS NT CALCULATOR

The computer has enormous potential to do arithmetic quickly and accurately. The Windows NT Calculator puts a hand-held calculator right on your screen. The Calculator, illustrated in Figure 6-1, has two views: Standard and Scientific. In this text, you will use the Standard Calculator. If your mathematical needs are more advanced, you most likely already know how to use the complex functions on the Scientific view.

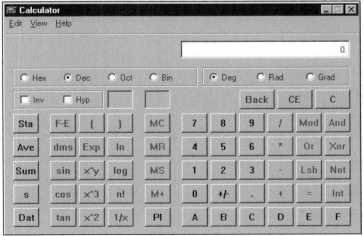

FIGURE 6-1

The Calculator: Standard and Scientific views

ENTERING NUMBERS

You can enter numbers with the keyboard or the mouse. Using the numeric keypad on the right side of your keyboard is usually easier. Press [Num Lock] before you start so the numeric keypad will enter numbers rather than activate the arrow keys. On most keyboards, an indicator light glows when [Num Lock] is active. Alternatively, you can use the mouse to click the digit buttons on the screen.

CLEARING THE CALCULATOR

The C (Clear) button sets the Calculator back to zero to start a new calculation. The CE (Clear Entry) button clears the last entry so you can rekey the entry without having to start over. The Back button deletes the last digit you typed. The MC (Memory Clear) button clears any number stored in the Calculator's memory.

MATHEMATICAL OPERATIONS

The (/) button is used for division; the (*) button, for multiplication; the (–) button, for subtraction; and the (+) button, for addition. Sometimes you must use (=) to display the results.

You can use on-screen Help to learn about other Calculator functions.

SELECTING THE CALCULATOR VIEW

In the following steps, you will switch back and forth between the Windows NT Calculator's Standard and Scientific views.

HANDS ON

1. Log on to Windows NT.
2. Choose Programs from the Start menu.
3. Highlight Accessories.

   The menu that appears shows the Accessories available to you.
4. Choose Calculator.

   The Standard Calculator window appears on the Desktop.
5. Click the Calculator window's View menu.

   Notice the check mark beside the Standard command.
6. Click Scientific.

   The Calculator window expands to the Scientific view.
7. Use the Calculator window's View menu to switch the window back to Standard view.

PERFORMING A MATHEMATICAL CALCULATION

In the following steps, you will use the Standard Calculator view to perform a mathematical calculation.

HANDS ON

1. Make sure the Calculator window is set for the Standard view.
2. Click 8.
3. Click *.
4. Click 6.
5. Click =.

   The answer to the mathematical statement (8x6=), 48, appears on the Calculator's display.

USING THE CALCULATOR'S MEMORY FEATURE

In the following steps, you will use the Calculator's Memory feature to continue the current calculation.

HANDS ON

1. Click the MS button.

   The displayed value is stored in memory, and an M appears in the Memory indicator box (above the MC button).

2. Click 5.

3. Click +/–.

4. Click M+.

   The displayed value, –5, is added to the value currently stored in memory.

5. Click CE.

6. Click MR.

   The value 43—the result of adding 48 and –5 in the Calculator's Memory—appears on the Calculator's display.

7. Click the MC button.

   The Calculator's Memory feature is cleared.

8. Click the Calculator window's Close button.

   The Calculator window no longer appears on the Desktop.

TEXT APPLETS

text editor A program which creates text files.

text file (or **unformatted file**) A data file containing text characters (letters, numbers, symbols, punctuation, spaces, and paragraph returns) without line, paragraph, or page formatting or typeface enhancements. Compare with *formatted file*.

Two basic kinds of text handling programs exist: text editors and word processors. A **text editor** creates unformatted or "plain vanilla" text files. **Text files**, or **unformatted files**, contain the characters you type and very little else. The NotePad accessory that you used in Lesson 5 is a text editor. When you save a NotePad document, its file type is Text.

Unformatted text files are used for the following purposes:

- To create and edit files that control computer startup functions and software settings.

- To transmit a file via modem. Since unformatted files are much smaller than formatted files, it is quicker and cheaper to send data as text files.

- To transfer text from one program to another program. This is most often necessary when dealing with non-Windows or DOS-based software or with incompatible computers or operating systems.

word processor A software application designed for writing, editing, and enhancing the appearance of text.

A **word processor** allows not only the production of text, but also the enhancement of the appearance or formatting of the document. Line spacing, page numbering, and word underlining are examples of formatting information a text editor does *not* include in its unformatted files. Word processor files can have a generic file type, such as Rich Text Document, or a program-specific file type such as a Word document.

USING WORDPAD

The WordPad applet is two programs in one: a text editor and a word processor. When you create a new WordPad document, your file type choice determines whether WordPad will be a text editor or a word processor. The New dialog box, as shown in Figure 6-2, lists three file type choices: Word 6 Document, Rich Text Document, and Text Document.

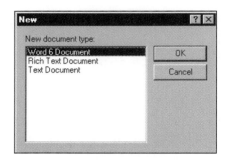

FIGURE 6-2
The New dialog box

The Word 6 Document format provides formatting features compatible with Microsoft's full-featured word processing application. The Rich Text Document format allows a file to be read (opened) by other word processing applications. The Text Document format creates an unformatted text document.

CREATING A TEXT FILE

In the following steps, you will use Windows NT WordPad accessory to create a text file.

HANDS ON

1. Insert your Student Data Disk into drive A: (or drive B:).

2. Choose Programs and then Accessories from the Start menu.

3. Choose WordPad from the Accessories menu.

The WordPad copyright box appears on the Desktop briefly, and then the WordPad window appears, as shown in Figure 6-3.

The WordPad window resembles the NotePad window with three significant additions. Below the menu bar is the toolbar, with buttons for WordPad's most common program commands. Under the toolbar is the **format bar,** with buttons for WordPad's most common formatting commands. Beneath the Format Bar is the **ruler,** which is used to format paragraphs of text.

format bar A row of buttons within a window, just below the toolbar, containing shortcuts for common formatting commands.

ruler A display of buttons and numbered tick marks beneath the WordPad format bar, which indicates measurements across the width of the document and is used to format paragraphs of text.

4. Compare your WordPad window with Figure 6-3. If your toolbar, format bar, or ruler are not displayed, turn them on one at a time from the View menu.

5. Size the WordPad window until you can see the entire toolbar.

The blinking insertion point below the ruler shows where text will appear as you type.

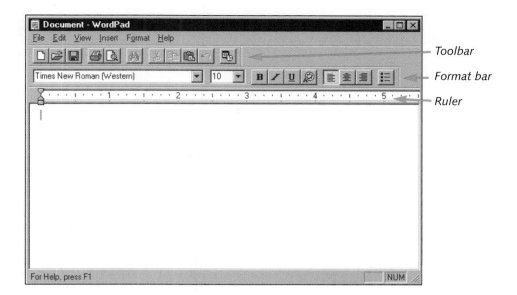

FIGURE 6-3

Blank WordPad document

6. Type the following lines of text:

Regarding contractors
The bottom line: How much will it cost?
How much of that cost can we reduce by performing the labor ourselves?

Your text should appear similar to the text shown in Figure 6-4.

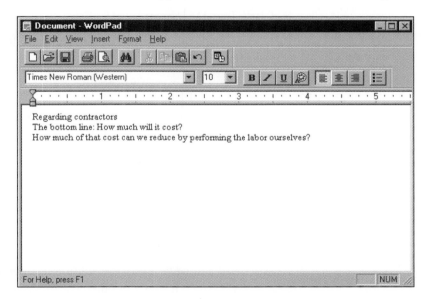

FIGURE 6-4

The WordPad document
with typed text

SAVING A TEXT FILE

In the following steps, you will name and save the text you've typed to your floppy disk as a Text document.

1. Click the Save button.

The Save As dialog box appears, as shown in Figure 6-5.

FIGURE 6-5

The Save As dialog box

2. Click the arrow in the Save In box.

The drop-down list of device options appears.

3. Click the icon for the drive that contains your Student Data Disk (drive A: or B:).

NOTE   *Make sure your Student Data Disk is in drive A: (or B:).*

4. Double-click the **WP-Files** folder.

5. Click the drop-down list arrow in the Save As Type box.

A drop-down list of file type options appears.

6. Click Text Document.

7. Double-click the word Document in the File Name text box to high-light it.

8. Type **A note to myself** in the File Name text box.

9. Click Save.

A dialog box asks if you really want a text document.

10. Click the Text Document button.

The document is stored in a text file named **A note to myself** on the selected disk.

OPENING A NEW DOCUMENT

WordPad can only have one document open at a time. In the following steps, you will open a new document in the WordPad window, thereby closing **A note to myself**.

1. Click the New button on the WordPad toolbar.

The New dialog box appears, with the default file type, Word 6 document.

2. Click OK.

A new, blank document replaces the previously displayed text stored in the text file you created.

OPENING AN EXISTING DOCUMENT

In the following steps, you will open the text document you created previously and saved in the file named **A note to myself.**

1. Click the Open button.

The Open dialog box appears, as shown in Figure 6-6.

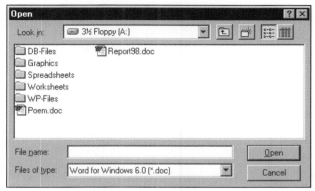

FIGURE 6-6

The Open dialog box

2. Choose the Text Documents (*.txt) option from the Files Of Type drop-down list.

3. Double-click the **WP-Files** folder.

4. Double-click the file name **A note to myself.**

The text stored in the selected file appears in the WordPad window.

EDITING EXISTING TEXT

In the following steps, you will modify an existing text document and save the changes.

1. Make sure the text document in the file **A note to myself** appears in the WordPad window.

2. Double-click the word *Regarding* in the first line of the document.

Double-clicking a word selects it. The word and the space character that follows it are highlighted.

3. Type **Ask all bidding**

NOTE   *Be sure to include a single space character after the word* bidding.

The new text replaces the existing text.

4. Press End and type : (a colon).

5. Select the phrase *The bottom line:,* including the space character that follows the colon.

6. Press Delete.

The selected text is deleted, and the rest of the text in the paragraph shifts. The document should appear similar to the one shown in Figure 6-7.

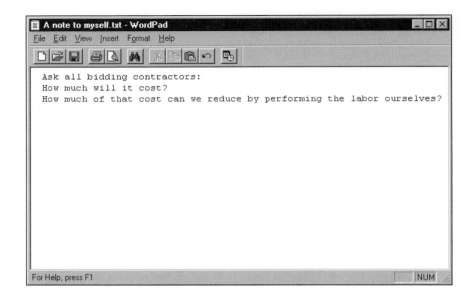

```
A note to myself.txt - WordPad                              _ □ ×
File  Edit  View  Insert  Format  Help

  Ask all bidding contractors:
  How much will it cost?
  How much of that cost can we reduce by performing the labor ourselves?




For Help, press F1                                          NUM
```

FIGURE 6-7
*The modified
text document*

 7. Click the Save button.

The modified version of the file is stored on disk.

N O T E *When you are working on a document, you should save your work every few minutes. If a power loss or a software or hardware problem causes the computer or program to malfunction, only the information you have not yet saved on disk is lost.*

PRINTING A TEXT DOCUMENT

In the following steps, you will print the text document you've created, modified, and saved.

 1. Make sure the printer connected to your system is turned on, is ready to print, has paper, and that the paper is aligned properly.

 2. Click the Print button.

The text in the WordPad window is sent to the printer. After a few moments, the printer should begin printing the document.

3. Click the WordPad window's Close button.

The WordPad window no longer appears on the Desktop.

MODIFYING A WORD FOR WINDOWS DOCUMENT FILE

WordPad's Word for Windows 6.0 Document default format option gives you a mini-version of a word processing program.

The format bar lets you select the fonts (the style and size of lettering) and line appearance (centering a line of text, for example). The ruler is used to set tabs and margins. These features allow you to enhance the appearance of text and paragraphs. Formatting a document refers to applying fonts, indenting or aligning paragraphs, and using other features to make it more appealing to readers. Such embellishments in a **formatted file** can make the document more attractive and easier to read.

formatted file A document containing elements that enhance the appearance of text, paragraphs, and other objects, in order to make the document more attractive and understandable. Compare with *text file*.

word wrap A word processing feature that automatically breaks lines at the right margin or right side of a window as you type.

Appearances aside, formatted files change the way you type. A feature called **word wrap** controls where lines of text end. As you type a paragraph, you can ignore the right margin. When text no longer fits on the current line, it automatically continues on a new line; you just continue typing.

N O T E   *If you select the Rich Text Document format option, the format bar and ruler do not appear. However, you can display these screen tools by using the View menu.*

OPENING A WORD FOR WINDOWS DOCUMENT FILE

In the following steps you will use Windows NT WordPad accessory program to open a document stored in Word for Windows 6.0 file format.

HANDS ON

1. Open WordPad.

 2. Click the Open button.

The Open dialog box appears.

3. If necessary, select drive A: (or drive B:) on the Look In drop-down list and choose Word for Windows 6.0 from the Files Of Type drop-down list.

4. Double-click the **WP-Files** folder.

5. Click the file named **Letter**, and then click Open.

The document stored in the **Letter** file appears in the WordPad window.

FORMATTING EXISTING TEXT

In the following steps, you will format selected text in the active document and then save the changes.

HANDS ON

1. Maximize the WordPad window, if necessary.

2. Click the down scroll arrow 10 times to scroll the line *Dear Ms. Canyon* to the top of the window.

 3. Point to the left of the *p* in *proposal document.*

The pointer becomes a right-pointing arrow.

4. Click.

The line highlights. When you click once to the left of a line of text, the entire line highlights.

5. Drag straight down to select the three lines, as shown in Figure 6-8.

You must select text before you can format it.

6. Click the WordPad window's Format menu.

The Format menu appears.

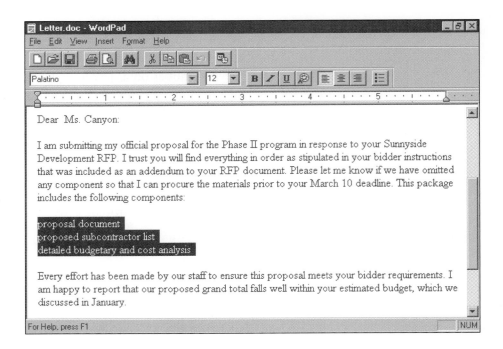

FIGURE 6-8
Selected lines

7. Click Bullet Style.

The selected lines are formatted as bullet paragraphs, each preceded by a bullet character (•).

8. Scroll to the bottom of the document. (Drag the vertical scroll box to the bottom of the scroll bar.)

9. Triple-click (click three times quickly) anywhere in the paragraph that begins *Thank you again....*

The paragraph highlights.

- A single click moves the insertion point to that location.

- A double-click selects the word under the pointer.

- A triple-click selects the paragraph under the pointer.

10. Press Delete.

The selected paragraph is deleted from the document.

11. Select the company name, *Woody Glenn*, in the letterhead.

12. Click the Bold button on the format bar.

The selected text formats with the Bold attribute, the text becomes heavier.

13. Select the Save button.

The latest changes are saved to the document stored in **Letter**.

PRINTING THE FORMATTED DOCUMENT

In the following steps, you will print the active formatted document and close the WordPad window.

HANDS ON

1. Make sure the printer connected to your system is turned on, is ready to print, has paper, and that the paper is aligned properly.

2. Click the Print button.

   The printer prints one copy of the **Letter** file.

3. Close the WordPad window.

USING PAINT

If a picture is worth a thousand words, think of the pages you save by adding a graphic to explain or complement your written text. The Paint applet in Windows NT lets you create or edit a picture using a variety of tools. Figure 6-9 identifies some of the major parts of the Paint window.

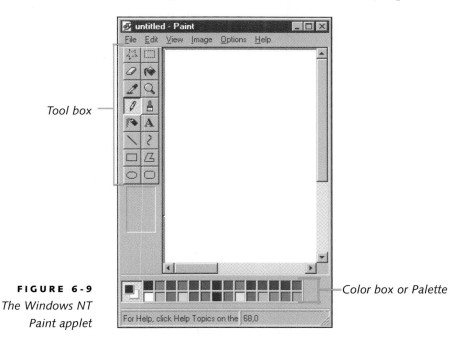

Tool box —

— Color box or Palette

FIGURE 6-9
*The Windows NT
Paint applet*

THE PAINT TOOL BOX

tool box An area in the Windows NT Paint accessory window containing icons representing the tools used to create an image.

On the left of the Paint window is the **tool box**. The tool box contains the tool buttons that you use to build an image. To use a tool, click its button. Table 6-4 explains each of the Tool icons.

When you choose certain Tool icons, other choices may appear below the tool box, allowing you to pick the shape, size, and other characteristics of the selected tool.

TABLE 6-4: TOOL ICONS

ICON	NAME	FUNCTION
	Free-Form Select	Lets you choose an irregularly shaped part of the painting to copy, move, or edit.
	Select	Lets you choose a rectangular part of the painting to copy, move, or edit.
	Eraser/Color Eraser	Erases a part of the painting.
	Fill With Color	Fills an enclosed area with the selected color.
	Pick Color	Selects a color from the painting.
	Magnifier	Zooms in on a part of the painting for detailed work or examination.
	Pencil	Draws a thin free-form line or shape.
	Brush	Draws a brush stroke of the selected brush shape and size.
	Airbrush	Sprays the selected color onto the painting.
	Text	Lets you add text of varying styles and sizes directly into your painting.
	Line	Draws a straight line of the selected width.
	Curve	Draws a curved line of the selected width.
	Rectangle	Creates a rectangle of the selected line width and color.
	Polygon	Creates a multi-sided shape of the selected line width and color.
	Ellipse	Creates an oval using the selected line width and color.
	Rounded Rectangle	Creates a rounded rectangle using the selected line width and color.

COLOR SELECTION

Color box (or **palette**) A device at the bottom of the Paint window that contains a set of colors displayed in small squares, which can be selected to change a shape's color.

On the bottom of the Paint window is the **Color box**. The Color box contains a series of squares of colors. These color choices are called the **palette**. To select the color with which you want to draw or fill, click the color in the Color box. To select a color from one already in the painting, use the Pick Color icon and click the desired color in the drawing.

You will use the Paint accessory to create, edit, and store a graphic image in a file.

HANDS ON

1. Choose Programs and then Accessories from the Start menu.

2. Click Paint.

The Paint window appears on the Desktop. The Pencil tool is chosen.

3. Click the Ellipse tool.

Its functional description appears in the status bar.

4. Click each of the tools on the tool box to read the names and functional descriptions.

5. Click the Pencil tool.

6. Point to the upper-left corner of the Paint document window.

The pointer is shaped like a pencil, your current painting tool. The position indicator at the bottom of the document window reflects the number of pixels from the upper-left corner of the window. For example, 10,12 means the pointer is 10 pixels from the left edge and 12 pixels down from the top of the window. Each **pixel** is one screen dot.

pixel Short for picture element; the smallest dot you can draw on the screen and the smallest unit that images on the screen consist of.

7. Maximize the Paint window.

8. Without pressing the mouse button, roll the pointer around the document window.

Notice that the position indicator changes to reflect the pointer's changing position.

9. Press the mouse button to drag the pointer around the window.

The Pencil tool creates a free-form line.

10. Choose Select All from the Edit menu.

Select All activates all the pixels in your window so that you can copy, move, delete, or modify them.

11. Press Delete.

The screen clears.

DRAWING WITH PAINT

Now you will use some tools to begin your drawing.

HANDS ON

1. Make sure you have a clear Paint window.

2. Use the Pencil tool to draw a flower, such as the one shown in Figure 6-10.

NOTE   *You may find it difficult to draw with the mouse. Graphic artists use specialized input devices to draw on the computer.*

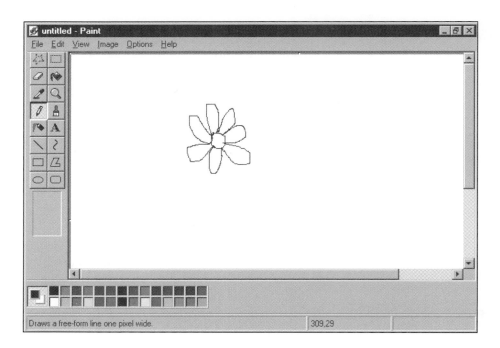

FIGURE 6-10

Pencil drawing of a flower

3. Click the green box in the Color box.

Green is now the selected color for any lines you paint.

 4. Click the Line tool.

The Line tool is selected and its line width options appear near the bottom of the toolbar.

 5. Point to the document window.

The pointer changes shape to become a cross pointer.

6. Click the bottom (thickest) line in the line width selector.

7. Point to the center of the flower.

8. Drag the mouse down to draw a thick green line.

Now you have a stem for your flower, as shown in Figure 6-11.

FILLING ENCLOSED AREAS

In the following steps, you will use the Fill With Color tool to fill contained areas in your image.

HANDS ON

 1. Choose the Fill With Color tool.

The pointer takes the shape of a spilling paint can. The drip of paint to the pointer's left is its active or "hot" spot.

2. Choose a color for your petals.

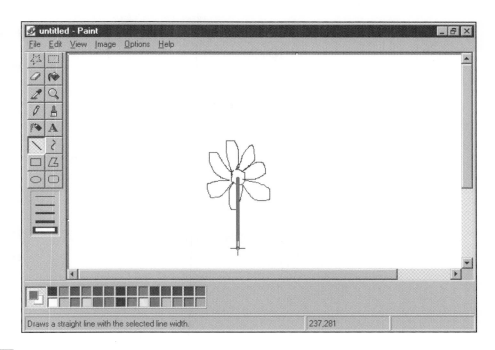

FIGURE 6-11
Stem added to flower

WARNING   *Before you click something, be sure that this hot spot is inside an enclosed area. Otherwise, your entire background will fill with color.*

3. Click one of the enclosed petals.

The enclosed area fills with the color you chose.

NOTE   *If the entire background fills with your chosen color, choose Undo from the Edit menu to try again.*

4. Choose a different color, and fill another enclosed area.

5. Use the procedure described in step 4 to fill each petal in your flower. Your flower should look something like the one shown in Figure 6-12.

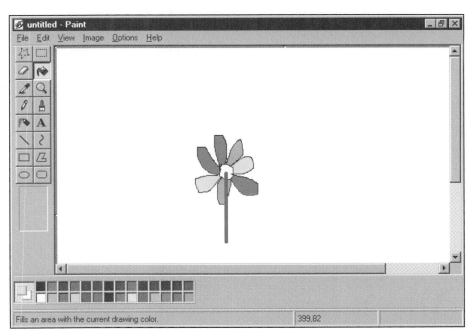

FIGURE 6-12
The image with color-filled petals

MOVING AND COPYING PART OF A DRAWING

You can move and copy parts of your drawing as long as you select the object first.

HANDS ON

1. Click the Select tool.

2. Point above and to the left of your flower.

3. Drag down and right diagonally to enclose your entire flower.

As you drag the mouse, a selection rectangle like the one shown in Figure 6-13 appears. All the pixels inside the rectangle are selected.

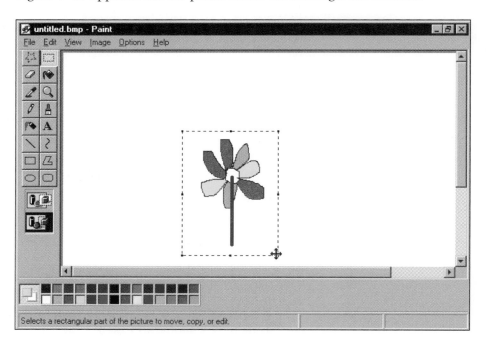

FIGURE 6-13
Flower selected

4. Point inside the selection rectangle.

The pointer changes shape to become a four-headed arrow. This pointer shape tells you that you can drag the rectangle to a new screen location.

5. Drag the selection to the left side of the screen.

As you drag, the image inside the selection rectangle moves.

6. Make sure the flower is still selected.

7. Press Ctrl .

8. Drag the flower to the right.

9. Release the mouse button.

A second flower is copied.

10. Continue to press Ctrl, drag, and release the button to fill your screen with flowers, as shown in Figure 6-14.

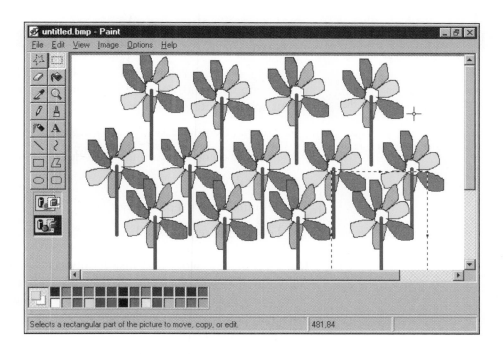

FIGURE 6-14
*Flowers copied all
over screen*

SAVING AND PRINTING THE IMAGE

In the following steps, you will name, save, and print your image. Then
you will close the Paint window.

**HANDS
ON**

1. Choose Save from the Paint window's File menu.

The Save As dialog box appears.

NOTE   *If you save an untitled document, Windows NT displays the Save As dialog box so that
you can locate and name the document.*

2. Be sure the Save In box displays the correct location (drive) of your
Student Data Disk or work disk.

3. Double-click the **Graphics** folder.

4. Activate the File Name text box, if necessary, and type **Flower Painting**
as the file name.

5. Click Save.

The image is saved and stored in a file named **Flower Painting**.

6. Be sure the printer connected to your system is turned on, is ready, has
paper, and that the paper is properly aligned.

7. Choose Print from the File menu.

The Print dialog box appears.

8. Click OK.

The image is sent to the printer and begins printing after a few moments.

9. Close the Paint window.

UNDERSTANDING COMMUNICATIONS ACCESSORIES

e-mail Another name for electronic mail, information that is exchanged between two computers via telephone lines or network connections.

The Communications accessories included in Windows NT let you and your computer send and receive **e-mail** (electronic mail) or faxes, which means sending information between your computer and:

- Another computer on the same network
- Another computer through a modem
- A fax device
- An intelligent telephone system

Few computers have all of the Windows NT communications accessories installed. Network users may install only network-specific accessories. Users not on a network may install only fax- and modem-related accessories. An individual who has both a desktop and laptop computer may install accessories that help coordinate the files on the two computers. For more information on these accessories, refer to the Help screen in Windows NT.

ACCESSING THE INTERNET

Internet A collection of computers linked together into a huge network.

modem Hardware that transfers data by converting computer signals that can be transmitted over a telephone line.

video conferencing Exchanging audio and video conversations electronically.

backbone Computers that make up the Internet.

Internet service providers (or **ISPs**) Companies that provide Internet access to users for a monthly or an annual fee.

online services Companies that include Internet access as a part of their own proprietary offerings.

browser A software package that lets the user access the major components of the Internet, such as the World Wide Web, e-mail, and so on.

World Wide Web (or **Web**) Screens of graphical information on the Internet controlled by companies, organizations, and individuals with a special interest to share.

The **Internet** is a collection of computers linked together into a huge network. Begun to enable scientists, researchers, and governments to share information, the Internet has grown to include users of diverse interests. The Internet consists of several components that allow the exchange of different kinds of information, such as files, electronic mail, electronic conversation, and so on. Each of these exchanges requires the user to have hardware and software to access the Internet.

Most individual users have a **modem** connected to a telephone line that carries signals between their computer and the Internet. Network users may share modems with other users. Faster connections use more expensive technology that not only transfers files faster but also allows for the exchange of audio and video conversations—known as **video-conferencing**.

Some large businesses and universities are part of the Internet **backbone**—the computers that make up the Internet. Other users must connect to the Internet indirectly, through **Internet service providers (ISPs)** or **online services**. Internet service providers charge a monthly or an annual fee to connect your computer to the Internet. Online services, such as America Online and Compuserve, include Internet access as a part of their own proprietary offerings.

To share information over the Internet and to explore all components of the Internet, you need appropriate software called a **browser**. The two most widely used browsers are Microsoft Internet Explorer and Netscape Navigator (a part of a larger software package called Netscape Communicator). Unlike the accessories you saw earlier in this lesson, Internet Explorer and Netscape Navigator are full-featured programs.

Many individuals feel that the most exciting component of the Internet is the **World Wide Web**, or the **Web** for short. The Web consists of screens, or **Web pages**, of information controlled by almost anyone with a special

Web pages Screens that display information on the Web. Many Web pages contain text, graphics, animation, sound, and video.

Web site Specific location of pages on the World Wide Web. A Web site has an address, or URL.

Universal Resource Locator (URL) Address of a Web site.

interest to share with others. Web pages can contain text, graphics, animation, sound, and video. Companies advertise products on the Web and may even sell the products directly to the user. Individuals create their own Web pages for a variety of reasons. Much of the Web is unregulated—check your source before relying on the information you see on the Web.

To find a specific location, or **Web site**, you must know its Web address, called the **Universal Resource Locator**, or **URL**. URLs are listed in magazine, newspaper, and television advertisements, on boxes of software packages, and within many help screens on your computer. **Search engines** let you find pages of interest by entering **keywords**. Much of the Web is in a constant state of flux—addresses and pages change daily. Search engines let you find a Web site that has moved since your last access.

EXPLORING THE WORLD WIDE WEB

In the following exercise, you will access the Internet's World Wide Web using your browser.

N O T E

Many different ways exist to connect to the Internet. Many computers connect automatically when you launch the browser; other systems require you to use the Dial-up Networking program first (click the Start button, Programs, Accessories, Dial-up Networking). You may need to contact your Network Administrator, instructor, lab assistant, or Internet service provider for specific instructions to connect to the Internet.

HANDS ON

1. Launch your browser and connect to the Internet.

Your browser will load and display your default or home page. The document window displays the home page—which may be set by your Network Administrator or Internet service provider. Figure 6-15 shows the Microsoft Internet Explorer window. If you are using another browser, your window may be similar to the figure.

search engine A company that lists Web sites. The user enters a keyword and the search engine lists sites that most nearly match it.

keyword Word or phrase used to define or narrow a search.

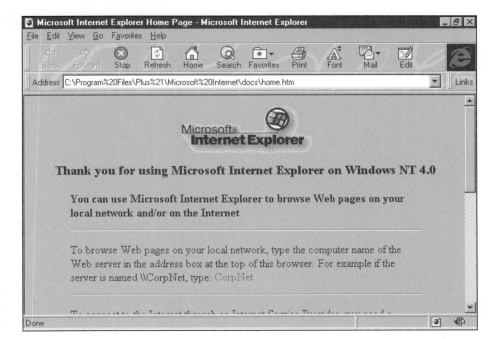

FIGURE 6-15
Microsoft Internet Explorer window

N O T E

If your connection to the Internet is already active, you will jump directly to your home page. If your connection is not active, you will see the Sign In or Connect To dialog box, first allowing you to connect to the Internet. If you receive an error message telling you that no connection has been established, run the Dial-up Networking accessory to connect to your ISP.

2. Click the Address text box above the document window.

N O T E

home page The main page of a World Wide Web site which usually includes links to other pages at that site.

The text box is called Location in Netscape Navigator.

The **home page** address is highlighted.

3. Type **http://www.glencoe.com** and press Enter.

After a short pause, you should see the Glencoe/McGraw-Hill home page as shown in Figure 6-16.

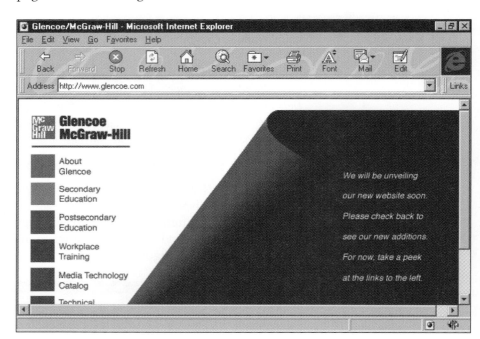

FIGURE 6-16
Glencoe/McGraw-Hill home page

N O T E

Be patient! Many factors affect the speed of the connection to the Internet and Web sites; sometimes you will connect instantly and other times it will take several minutes. Some of the factors that affect the connection time include the speed of your modem, the amount of "traffic" on your ISP, and the number of people seeking access to the site.

The Internet is a dynamic world. Site addresses and pages change frequently. Some owners update their pages constantly, so don't be surprised if you look at the same Web page tomorrow and the links have changed or the page looks different.

4. Move your mouse pointer over the home page.

links Locations on a Web page that you click to jump to other locations or parts of the Internet.

Your mouse pointer changes to a hand-shape when you pass over certain text or graphics areas. These locations are called **links**. When you click a link, your browser jumps to (a) another location on the Web page; (b) another page at the current site; (c) another Web site; or (d) another part of the Internet, such as e-mail.

5. Click the About Glencoe link.

You are taken to another page at the current site.

 6. Click the Back button.

You return to the previous page.

7. Click other links to explore this Web site.

8. Close your browser and disconnect from the Internet.

W A R N I N G   *You may need to disconnect your modem manually (click the Start button, Programs, Accessories, Dial-up Networking, and Hangup).*

9. Log off your computer or complete the exercises for this lesson.

LESSON SUMMARY AND EXERCISES

After you complete this lesson, you should know how to do the following:

INTRODUCING WINDOWS NT ACCESSORIES

- Identify accessories belonging to general-purpose, communications, and multimedia categories.

USING THE WINDOWS NT CALCULATOR

- Distinguish between the Standard and Scientific calculator views.

- Use the Calculator applet to perform basic arithmetic in the Standard view.

INTRODUCING TEXT APPLETS

- Differentiate between two basic kinds of text handling programs: text editors, which produce text files that are unformatted, and word processors, which produce formatted text files.

USING WORDPAD

- Create text files using WordPad. Click the New button and select the Text Document format.

- Create formatted documents in WordPad. Click the New button and select the Word 6 Document format.

USING PAINT

- Select tools and options to create and save a Paint image.

UNDERSTANDING COMMUNICATIONS ACCESSORIES

- Recognize the accessories that let you send and receive information from your computer.

ACCESSING THE INTERNET

- Explore the World Wide Web using your Web browser.

NEW TERMS TO REMEMBER

After you complete this lesson, you should know the meaning of these terms:

accessories	links	Universal Resource Locator (URL)
applets	modem	video conferencing
backbone	multimedia	Web
browser	online services	Web pages
Color box	palette	Web site
e-mail	pixel	word processor
format bar	ruler	word wrap
formatted file	search engine	World Wide Web
home page	text editor	
Internet	text file	
Internet Service Providers (ISPs)	tool box	
keyword	unformatted file	

MATCHING EXERCISE

Match each of the terms with the definitions on the right:

TERMS	DEFINITIONS
1. accessories	**a.** Feature of word processors in which typed text automatically drops to the next line when the cursor reaches the right margin
2. applets	**b.** Pure, unenhanced text file
3. Color box	**c.** Device within the Windows NT Paint accessory that allows you to select from a variety of drawing tools
4. e-mail	
5. formatted file	**d.** Another term for accessory programs
6. palette	**e.** Another name for the Color box
7. pixel	**f.** Short for electronic mail, a means of transmitting written information via telephone lines between computers equipped with modems
8. tool box	
9. word wrap	**g.** A single dot on the computer screen
10. unformatted file	**h.** Ancillary programs for specific tasks that are included with the Windows NT operating system
	i. Device from which color options can be selected
	j. Document file that stores formatting characteristics—such as fonts, indentation, and so forth—along with text

COMPLETION EXERCISE

Fill in the missing word or phrase for each of the following:

1. The _____ feature in word processors allows you to type text without having to press [Enter] at the end of each line.

2. The tool box in the Windows NT _____ accessory allows you to select a variety of painting tools.

3. The WordPad accessory allows you to create, view, and edit both _____ files, which contain text only, and _____ files.

4. If you need to find the square root of a number, you can do so with the _____ accessory.

5. The Windows NT accessory that functions like a word processing program is called _____ .

6. You can find a Web site by using a search engine or by typing its _____ _____ _____ .

7. When creating or editing an image using the Paint accessory, you can choose from a variety of colors on the _____, also called the _____.

8. The joining of text, graphics, sound, and sometimes animation into the same application software package is called _____.

9. To send an e-mail message to another computer, you need to use one or more of the _____ accessories.

10. Small application programs provided with the Windows NT operating system are referred to as either a(n) _____ or a(n)_____ .

SHORT-ANSWER QUESTIONS

Write a brief answer to each of the following questions:

1. Why do operating systems often include accessory programs?

2. Differentiate between a text editor and a word processor.

3. What are the file types for WordPad documents? How do you choose the one you want?

4. Differentiate among the WordPad toolbar, format bar, and ruler.

5. How do you view or hide each of the screen elements in question 4?

6. Which Windows NT accessory might be used to create a logo for a personal letterhead?

7. How do you select part of a Paint document? Why might you do this?

8. In Paint, how do you change the thickness of a line you plan to create? How do you change its color?

9. In Paint, why does the Fill With Color tool sometimes color your entire background when you try to color a part of your painting? What steps should you take to correct this problem?

10. The Windows NT Communications accessories allow your computer to send and receive information between your computer and other devices. Which devices might you want to access from your system, and why? (You can answer hypothetically or actually.)

APPLICATION PROJECTS

Insert your Student Data Disk into drive A: (or drive B:). Perform the following actions to complete these projects:

1. Start the WordPad accessory program and maximize its window, if necessary. Open the document file named **Memo** in the **WP-Files** folder on your Student Data Disk. Position the insertion bar to the right of the tab space following the label *DATE:*, and type today's date. Highlight the name *Myra* and type your name. Next, highlight the word *administrative* in the memo's first body paragraph and delete it. Then display the WordPad window's format bar, if necessary; highlight the four lines that describe the budget allocation revisions; and then select the Bullets button on the format bar. Finally, save the revised memo in a new file named **NewMemo** in the **Memos** subfolder of your Student Data Disk. Your revised memo document should resemble the one shown in Figure 6-17. Print the document, and then close the WordPad accessory program.

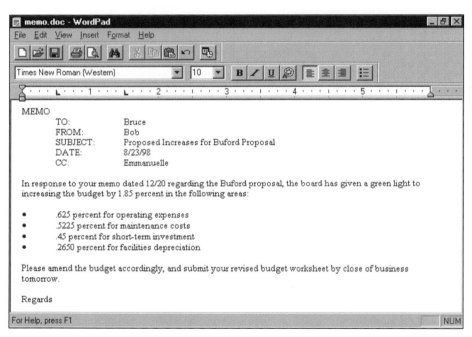

FIGURE 6-17

The revised memo for Application Project 1

2. Use the Calculator to determine the answers to the following arithmetic problems. Remember to clear the Calculator between each calculation.

    a. 4521 + 865 + 975 + 36 =

    b. 86.29 – 75.68 =

    c. 754891.562/829.67 =

    d. 126.75 * 94.38/69 =

3. Open the Paint accessory program's window. Use selected tools to create your own picture. Be creative; experiment with different shapes, options, and colors to create an attractive design.

4. Open the Paint accessory window. Open the image stored in the file named **Cupid** on your Student Data Disk. Use color palette selections and any tools you wish to enhance the image.

Save the changes in a file named **Heart**. Close the Paint window.

5. Open the WordPad accessory program. Write a note to a friend and format its text as you choose. Be experimental. Save the document in a file with the name of your friend in the **WP-Files** folder of your Student Data Disk. Print the note, and then close the WordPad window.

6. Launch your browser and connect to the Internet. Click the Search button and select a search engine to find information about (a) your school, (b) employment in a company you would like to work for, (c) a book you would like to purchase. Write down the results of your search, including the search engine you selected and the keyword or phrase that helped you locate the appropriate Web sites. Discuss the results of your research with other students in the class.

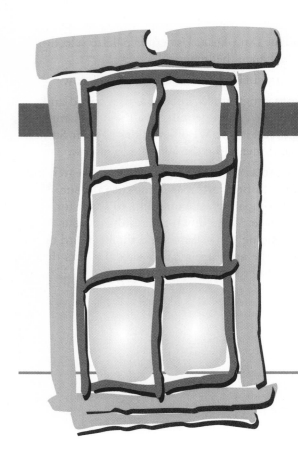

CONTROLLING

PRINTING

FEATURES

OBJECTIVES

After you complete this lesson, you will be able to do the following:

- *Control your print queue by deleting and pausing print jobs.*

- *View and select fonts to enhance your printed output.*

- *Use different sizes of paper available to your printer.*

- *Switch between portrait and landscape orientations.*

- *Choose the best resolution for your printed copy.*

CONTENTS

Managing Your Printer

Selecting and Using Fonts

Selecting Paper and Page Characteristics

Setting Printing Resolution

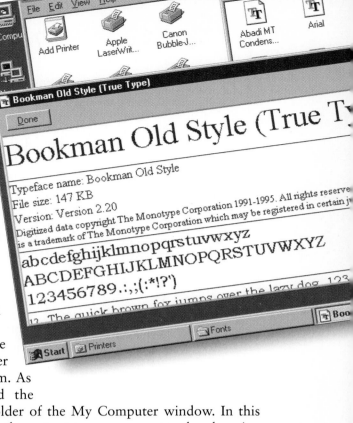

At one time computers were believed to be ushering in a paperless society. Although that era may come some day, today's computers can and do produce vast amounts of printed output. Whether you create junk mail, letters, brochures, or greeting cards, your output quality is dependent upon your operating system, application software, design choices, and printer.

In Lesson 3, you viewed some of the properties of the printer attached to your computer system. As you recall, you double-clicked the Printer icon from the Printers folder of the My Computer window. In this lesson, you will learn to manage the output to your computer by changing these properties and through other controls.

MANAGING YOUR PRINTER

When Windows was installed on your computer, information about the printer or printers available to your computer was stored.

Whenever an application (or mini-application) prints a document, a "soft" copy of the output is temporarily stored on the hard disk first. This process is called **print spooling**. It allows you to work on another project while the computer actually prints the **hard copy** of your document onto paper.

Without print spooling, you would have to wait until printing has ended to perform any other tasks with the computer. Because data is sent to the printer much more slowly than a computer can process data, you would have to wait a long time before you could resume your work.

print spooling Process of sending print jobs to a print queue so that printing can take place while the computer is used for other tasks.

hard copy Information that has been printed from its electronic, or "soft," form of storage on a computer, onto paper.

USING THE PRINT SPOOLER

Print spooling allows you to control your printer even after you "print" your work from the application window. Each print request sent to the print spool is placed in a print queue. The **print queue** is a list of print jobs waiting to be sent to a particular printer.

You can cancel or pause the jobs in the print queue. For example, if you send three documents to the queue, they do not have to be printed in the order they were sent. You can select individual jobs and pause or cancel them before they are sent to the printer. As a result, a long document doesn't have to tie up a printer. If you need to print a short memo immediately, you can pause the long document on the queue, print the short memo, and then resume printing the long document. You can even clear the entire print queue in one step—a technique known as **purging**.

print queue Temporary storage area in memory or on disk for data sent to a printer; in Windows NT, the name for a window showing active print jobs.

purging Canceling all jobs in a print queue.

OPENING YOUR PRINT QUEUE

In the following steps, you will open the window (queue) for the printer connected to your system. Begin by logging on to Windows NT and inserting your Student Data Disk in the appropriate drive.

HANDS ON

1. Choose Settings from the Start menu.

2. Choose the Printers folder.

3. Double-click the device icon labeled with the name of the printer connected to your system.

    Your printer's window appears.

4. Minimize your printer's window.

    Your print queue is minimized to a button but still available from the taskbar.

5. Close the Printers window.

STARTING WORDPAD AND PRINTING A DOCUMENT

In the following steps, you will start the WordPad accessory program, open a document file, and then print the document.

HANDS ON

1. Choose Programs and then Accessories from the Start menu.

2. Open the WordPad accessories program.

3. Click the Open button.

4. Select the correct disk location for your Student Data Disk, if necessary, and open the file named **Letter** in the **WP-Files** folder.

5. Click your printer's button on the taskbar.

    The print queue window opens on top of WordPad.

6. Tile the WordPad and print queue windows. (Click a blank spot on the taskbar with the right mouse button; choose Tile Horizontally from the shortcut menu.)

7. Activate the WordPad window.

8. Chose Print from the File menu.

    The Print dialog box appears, as shown in Figure 7-1.

9. Click OK.

    The document is sent to the printer. A message box appears, briefly, while the data is spooling. It identifies the spooling document and the target printer.

10. Without waiting for your document to print, go on to the next section.

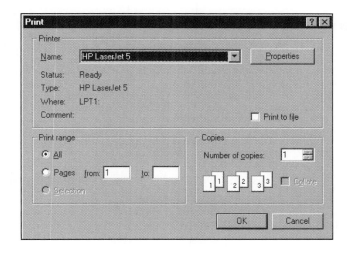

FIGURE 7-1

The Print dialog box

PAUSING A PRINT JOB

In the following steps, you will pause the print job you've just sent to the printer.

HANDS ON

1. Watch your printer's window. As you watch, the job you just sent will become listed in the print queue, as shown in Figure 7-2.

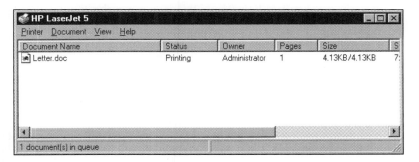

FIGURE 7-2

The printer window with a print job

2. Click the Printer menu, and then choose Pause Printing.

The current print job is paused, as indicated in the print queue. (You will learn how to resume printing shortly.)

OPENING AND PRINTING ANOTHER DOCUMENT

In the following steps, you will return to the WordPad window, open another document, and then send it to the printer.

HANDS ON

1. Click the WordPad window to activate it.

2. Click the Open button.

The Open dialog box appears.

3. Double-click the **Memo** file.

The document stored in the **Memo** file replaces the **Letter** document in the WordPad window.

4. Click the Print button.

The current document is sent directly to the print queue.

CANCELING A PRINT JOB

To cancel a print job, you delete its name from the print queue. In the following steps, you will select and delete a queued print job.

1. Click the second print job listed.

It highlights.

2. Choose Cancel Printing from the Document menu.

The selected print job is canceled.

3. Close the WordPad window and minimize your printer's window.

RESUMING PRINTING

In the following steps, you will activate the printer window and resume the paused print job.

1. Double-click the printer icon on the right side of the taskbar.

Notice that the print job appears in the window.

2. Click the print job to select it.

The selected print job highlights.

3. Click Pause Printing from the Printer menu.

The selected print job resumes printing.

4. Close the open window.

SELECTING AND USING FONTS

The appearance of printed text is greatly enhanced by using different styles for the characters that make up the text. Many of the first computer printers had only a single style of lettering. Hardware additions and cartridges became available to change the style on later printers. Most of today's dot-matrix, ink jet, bubble jet, and laser printers can print more than one style for characters in a single document without any changes to the hardware. This is accomplished within the software itself.

In the early days of personal computing, the characters viewed on the screen only approximated the look of the printed output. With the coming of WYSIWYG ("What You See Is What You Get"), however, on-screen and printed characters look alike.

Any text that is printed on paper appears in a font. A **font** is a set of characters that appear with a specific typeface, one or more attributes, and a specific size. A **typeface** is a family for type or printed characters that is determined by particular design or style characteristics. For instance, the Times New Roman typeface looks very different from the Helvetica typeface, as shown in Figure 7-3. In fact, these two examples demonstrate the two general categories for typefaces: serif and sans-serif.

A **serif typeface** like Times New Roman is adorned with little lines and curves on the tips, or strokes, of each character—the **serifs**. The text you're reading now is another example of a serif typeface. In general, serif typefaces

font A set of characters that appear with a specific typeface, one or more attributes, and a specific size.

typeface A specific design for a set of text characters which makes all the characters similar in appearance.

serif font A typeface whose characters have extra lines at the ends of the strokes which make text more readable; serif typefaces are generally used for paragraph text.

serif An extra line at the end of a text character stroke that is part of the character design.

sans serif A typeface whose characters lack extra lines at the ends of the strokes; sans serif typefaces are generally used for headings or display text.

are better suited for paragraph text because the little lines and curves help the eye to flow along each line more smoothly as the text is read. **Sans-serif** typefaces, like Helvetica, on the other hand, do not have these lines and curves. Their appearance is more block-like. Sans-serif typefaces generally work better for headings where reading ease is not as critical. Figure 7-3 illustrates several serif and sans-serif typefaces.

Serif Typefaces

Courier

Bookman

Times New Roman

Sans-Serif Typefaces

Arial

Helvetica

Century Gothic

FIGURE 7-3
Serif and sans-serif typefaces

attribute Enhancement or stylistic characteristic applied to text characters in a font, for example, bold, italic, and underlining.

weight An attribute applied to on-screen text or printed characters that influences the thickness of the characters and the spacing between them.

point (1) The action of pointing; (2) a unit of measurement equal to 1/72 inch that is used to describe the height of type and other elements on a printed page.

Attributes for typefaces include characteristics such as bold, italic, or underlining. These features enhance the appearance of a typeface. The **weight** of printed characters—that is, the thickness of the characters and the spacing between characters—is also an attribute that affects the appearance of typefaces. Thicker character strokes and/or less letter spacing can make typefaces appear heavier; thinner character strokes and/or more letter spacing can make typefaces appear lighter or more airy.

The size of printed characters is another element that makes up a font. The most common unit of measurement for typefaces is the **point**. One point is equal to $\frac{1}{72}$ inch, and points are used to express vertical measurement. A line of characters in a 12-point typeface occupies approximately $\frac{1}{6}$ inch vertically, because $\frac{12}{72}$ points equal $\frac{1}{6}$ inch. In general, body text appears in 10- to 12-point typefaces. Headlines and display type generally appear in bigger sizes, anywhere from 14 to 72 points or more.

When you put together a typeface, size, and one or more attributes, you have a font. For example, 12-point Courier, 10-point Times New Roman Bold, and 36-point Helvetica Condensed Italic are three fonts, but the term is frequently used to refer more generally to the entire font family, for example, Courier, Times New Roman, or Helvetica.

USING PRINTER FONTS

scaleable font Typeface that can be printed in a range of sizes.

Printers produce two types of fonts: scaleable and bitmap (nonscaleable) fonts. **Scaleable fonts** can be printed in a range of sizes. This means the user can select the point size from within the application. Windows NT provides several, scaleable True Type fonts (which appear with the TT icon beside their names in the Windows NT environment). True Type fonts are very desirable for a graphical user interface because they display the same way on screen as they do when printed on paper. Other manufacturers of scaleable, viewable fonts include Bitstream, Speedo, and Postscript. These fonts are supported by Windows NT and have their own file type icons.

bitmap font (or **nonscaleable font**) A typeface in which each character is composed of a dot pattern that dictates the shape and size of the font.

Bitmap fonts (nonscaleable) are usually built into the printer. Each character is composed of a dot pattern. Bitmap fonts are not scaleable because each size requires its own pattern. When you select a bitmap font from within your application software, Windows NT tries to match it with a similar screen font.

VIEWING AND PRINTING SAMPLE FONTS

In the following steps, you will view some of the font options available on your system, and then you will print a sampling of selected fonts.

HANDS ON

1. Choose Settings from the Start menu.

2. Click the Control Panel folder.

3. Scroll the Control Panel window, if necessary, to locate the Fonts folder.

4. Double-click the Fonts folder.

The Fonts window appears, as shown in Figure 7-4. Each font is contained in a separate file and represented by its own icon. True Type font icons have blue TT on their file icons; bitmap fonts have a red A.

FIGURE 7-4
The Fonts window

N O T E   *Fonts are customizable. You computer probably has a different set than the ones displayed in Figure 7-4.*

5. Double-click the Arial icon.

The Arial window appears with an informational and sample screen of the selected font, as shown in Figure 7-5.

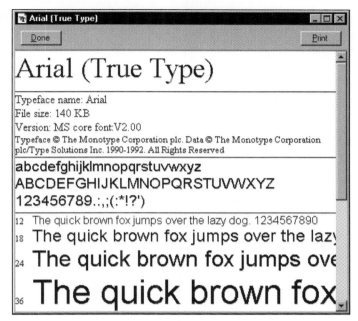

FIGURE 7-5
The Arial window

NOTE   *If the Arial (True Type) font is not available on your system, select another sans-serif option, such as Helvetica or MS Sans Serif.*

6. Scroll down the sample font window to see the screen display of larger-size Arial type.

Size samples, up to 72 points, appear in the window.

7. Click the Print button (and then OK if the Print dialog box appears).

The font sample is sent to the printer and printed.

8. Close the Arial (True Type) window.

PRINTING MORE SAMPLE FONTS

In the following steps, you will print two more font samples.

HANDS ON

1. Make sure the Fonts window is open.

2. Double-click the Courier New icon.

The Courier New window appears with a sample of the selected font.

NOTE   *If the Courier New font is not available on your system, select another serif option, such as Times New Roman, Courier, or Bookman.*

3. Click Print.

The font sample is sent to the printer and printed.

4. Close the window.

5. Open the font sample window for another font of your choice. Print the sample, and then close the window.

6. Close the Fonts and Control Panel windows.

SELECTING PAPER AND PAGE CHARACTERISTICS

In addition to fonts, print quality is also affected by page setup options that control the size, source, and orientation of the paper.

FEEDING THE PAPER

The appearance of your printed output varies widely depending on your printer and the kind of paper on which it can print. Some printers can accept many different sizes of paper, while others are more limited. Usually, dot-matrix printers use either tractor-fed paper (paper with holes on the sides by which the paper is pulled through the printer) or paper fed into the printer manually, one sheet at a time.

Laser, ink jet, and bubble jet printers use separate sheets of paper stored in trays. Some trays hold only one size of paper; others hold several sizes. If your printer holds more than one tray at a time, you can print various sized pages within the same document. Otherwise, you have to change trays or feed the paper manually.

The Paper Source list in the Default Document Properties dialog box lets you select the location of the paper to be used.

CHOOSING PAPER SIZE

Not all documents must be printed on 8½ × 11-inch paper. Most printers can accommodate a variety of paper sizes. The Page Setup tab in the Default Document Properties dialog box for your printer lists available paper sizes. Figure 7-6 shows the Paper Size options. Some of the most popular paper sizes are listed in Table 7-1.

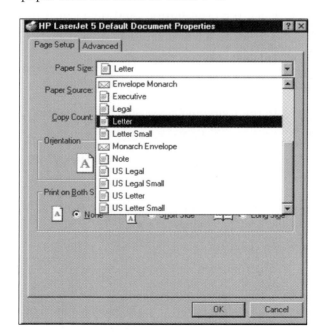

FIGURE 7-6

Some paper options in the Default Document Properties dialog box

TABLE 7-1: PAPER SIZES

SIZE (W × H)	DESCRIPTION
8½ × 11 in.	Most common paper size. Also called Letter.
8½ × 14 in.	Longer than Letter paper. Also called Legal.
7½ × 10½ in.	Executive size. Slightly narrower and shorter than Letter paper.
3⅞ × 8⅞ in.	Envelope (#9).

SELECTING THE ORIENTATION

portrait orientation A page layout option in which text and graphics are printed across the shorter dimension of a page.

landscape orientation A page layout option which prints text and graphics across the longer dimension of a page.

Orientation refers to the layout of the image in relation to the dimensions of the page. You can print your document using one of two orientations—portrait or landscape. **Portrait orientation** is what we usually think of as "normal" orientation. That is, text and graphics are printed across the shorter width and down the longer length of the page (for example, 8½ × 11 inches). In **landscape orientation** the text and graphics are printed across the longer width and down the shorter length (for example, 11 × 8½ inches). Figure 7-7 shows these orientations.

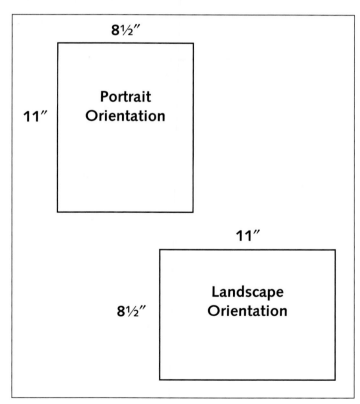

FIGURE 7-7

Portrait and landscape orientations

SETTING PAPER SIZE AND ORIENTATION

In the following steps, you will experiment with various Page Setup options.

HANDS ON

1. Open the Printers folder from Settings on the Start menu.

   The Printers window appears.

2. Double-click the icon named for the printer connected to your system.

3. Click Document Defaults from the Printer menu.

   The Default Document Properties window appears, with printer-specific options to choose from. (Your Default Document Properties window may show a different group of options than the ones shown in Figure 7-6.)

4. Click the Page Setup tab.

   The set of Page Setup options appears, as shown in Figure 7-6. Paper Size is the first option.

5. Click the drop-down arrow to view the Paper Size options.

   Clicking a Paper Size option makes that the default paper size. Do not change the default.

6. Click the Landscape radio button.

7. Click OK.

   You have just changed the default orientation to landscape. The next document you print will now appear in landscape orientation.

8. Close your printer's window.

PRINTING A DOCUMENT

In the following steps, you will drag-and-drop a document onto your Printer icon to print the document.

HANDS ON

1. Double-click the My Computer window to open it.

2. Open the drive containing your Student Data Disk.

3. Tile the open windows vertically.

4. Scroll the Student Data Disk window, if necessary, to locate the **Cupid** file icon.

5. Make sure the list of installed printers (icons) appears in the Printers window.

6. Drag the **Cupid** file icon to the icon for the printer attached to your system. Release the mouse button when the icon and name highlight.

   The file is sent to the printer. It may take a few minutes for the data to be spooled and the printer to begin printing. When the image prints, it should be positioned for landscape orientation, if your printer supports it.

RESTORING PAGE ORIENTATION

In the following steps, you will return the page orientation setting to portrait. Then you will close all Desktop windows.

HANDS ON

1. Double-click the icon, if necessary, for the printer connected to your system.

2. Choose Document Defaults from the Printer menu.

The Default Document Properties window for the printer appears on the Desktop.

3. Click the Page Setup tab, if necessary.

4. Click the Portrait radio button.

5. Click OK.

6. Close all open windows.

SETTING PRINTING RESOLUTION

resolution A measurement of image quality usually applied to printers and computer monitors; printer resolution is typically expressed in dots per inch (dpi).

draft Lowest resolution print quality setting, typically used for printing rough drafts rapidly.

letter quality Highest resolution print quality setting, typically used for printing final drafts.

Almost every printer produces text and images graphically—that is, as a series of dots. The more dots that can be printed in a given area, the higher the **resolution**. Many printers can print at several resolutions. As a rule, the higher the resolution, the clearer the hard copy appears and the longer it takes to print. High resolution printing also uses more ink. **Draft** is the lowest resolution, while **letter quality** is the term used for the highest resolution. You should print in draft mode when the quality of the output is not important or when you want a quick printout to proofread or edit. Use letter quality to create more attractive and readable hard copy.

Resolution is measured in the number of dots per inch (dpi). Sometimes resolution for a dot-matrix printer is expressed as two numbers that correspond to the number of dots printed horizontally and vertically in a square inch. Thus, a resolution of 180 × 180 means up to 180 dots can be printed horizontally or vertically in an inch. Laser printers usually express resolution with a single number in dots per inch (dpi) units, such as 600 or 1200 dpi.

CHANGING PRINT RESOLUTION

In the following steps, you will print two samples, each in a different resolution.

NOTE   *This activity is only meaningful if your printer supports multiple resolutions.*

HANDS ON

1. Open the Printers window.

2. Double-click the icon of the printer connected to your system.

3. Choose Document Defaults from the Printer menu.

Your printer's Default Document Properties dialog box appears.

4. Click the Advanced tab.

5. Click the Resolution option.

If your printer is a dot-matrix printer, then a set of Graphics options appears that is similar to the set shown in Figure 7-8. If your printer is a laser printer, then a set of Graphics options similar to the one shown in Figure 7-9 appears.

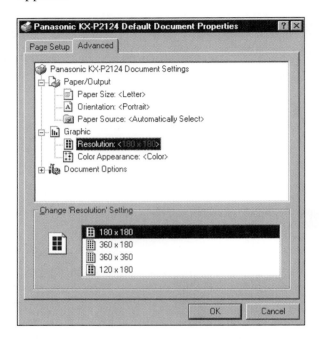

FIGURE 7-8

Graphic options for a standard dot-matrix printer

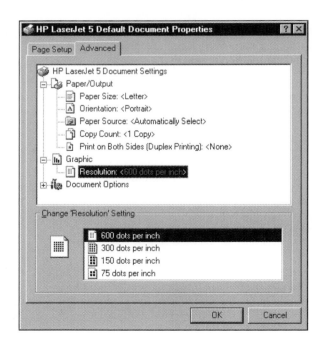

FIGURE 7-9

Graphic options for a standard laser printer

6. If your printer is a dot-matrix printer, select the lowest numbers for the Resolution setting; if your printer is a laser or ink jet printer, make sure the Resolution setting is set for the lowest dpi.

7. Click OK.

8. Set up your Desktop so that the Printers window and the window for the drive that contains your Student Data Disk are both visible.

9. Drag the **Star** file icon to the icon for the printer connected to your system. Release the mouse button when the icon highlights.

   The selected file is sent to the printer.

10. Reset your printer to its highest resolution. Then print the **Star** file again and compare the results.

N O T E   *If you are using a laser printer with 600 dpi resolution, return the printer resolution to 600 dpi resolution, as shown in Figure 7-9.*

11. Close all open windows.

12. If you want to quit your work on the computer, log off. Otherwise, leave your computer in its current status, and complete the exercises for this lesson.

LESSON SUMMARY AND EXERCISES

After you complete this lesson, you should know how to do the following:

MANAGING YOUR PRINTER

- Send the output of a WordPad document to your printer.
- Pause, resume, and print documents from your printer's window.

SELECTING AND USING FONTS

- View and display typefaces available on your computer system through the Fonts window.

SELECTING PAPER AND PAGE CHARACTERISTICS

- Change the paper size and print orientation of your output through your printer's Default Document Properties window.

SETTING PRINTING RESOLUTION

- Print output in both draft and high resolutions through your printer's Default Document Properties window.

NEW TERMS TO REMEMBER

After you complete this lesson, you should know the meaning of these terms:

attribute	letter quality	resolution
bitmap font	nonscaleable font	sans serif
draft	point	scaleable font
font	portrait orientation	serif
hard copy	print queue	serif font
landscape orientation	print spooling	typeface
	purging	weight

MATCHING EXERCISE

Match each of the terms with the definitions on the right:

TERMS	DEFINITIONS
1. draft	**a.** Page orientation in which an image is printed across the 8½-inch width of an 8½ × 11-inch page
2. font	
3. landscape	**b.** Process in which data sent for printer output is first sent to special files on the hard disk
4. point	
5. portrait	**c.** Graphic quality of printed images determined by the number of dots per square inch that make up the image
6. print queue	
7. print spooling	**d.** Appearance of printed characters based on a specific typeface, size, and one or more specific attributes
8. resolution	
9. scaleable font	**e.** Low-resolution print quality
10. typeface	**f.** Typeface, one or more attributes, and weight that can be printed in any size by a printer
	g. Family of design or style characteristics for printed characters
	h. Unit of measurement for printed characters that equals ¹⁄₇₂ inch
	i. Page orientation in which an image is printed across the 11-inch width of an 8½ × 11-inch page
	j. Special area that stores print jobs temporarily and that allows for manipulating them before the data is sent to the printer

COMPLETION EXERCISE

Fill in the missing word or phrase for each of the following questions:

1. The ability to type a memo in a word processing application while a worksheet is being printed by the printer connected to the system is possible because of Windows NT's _____.

2. _____ is a one-step technique for clearing the entire print queue.

3. Characters appearing in 12-point Helvetica Bold Italic are an example of a(n) _____.

4. As a general rule, _____ fonts are better suited for body text because they are easier for the eye to follow as it reads the text.

5. A higher point size number means a(n) _____ font.

6. Letter quality means a(n) _____ resolution than draft quality.

7. Bitmap fonts are generally built into _____ printers.

8. _____ orientation means that text and graphics are printed across the length of a standard, 8½ × 11-inch page.

9. Bold text has a heavier _____ than non-bold text.

10. The computer's printed output is known as _____.

SHORT-ANSWER QUESTIONS

Write a brief answer to each of the following questions:

1. List and define the elements or characteristics that make up a font.

2. List the advantages that print spooling has over sending data directly to a printer.

3. Describe briefly a situation in which using draft quality for printed output would be preferable and a situation in which using letter quality would be preferable.

4. As a general rule, which kind of typeface, serif or sans serif, would work best for large headlines? Why?

5. Briefly describe the procedure that you can use to cancel a print job.

6. Why might you want to cancel a print job?

7. Differentiate between scaleable and nonscaleable fonts.

8. How do you make and print font sample sheets?

9. What is the difference between portrait and landscape orientation? What steps do you follow to change default orientation?

10. How do you view and display the typefaces available to your system?

APPLICATION PROJECTS

Insert your Student Data Disk into drive A: (or drive B:). Perform the following actions to complete these projects:

1. Open the WordPad accessory program, and then open the file named **Memo**. Use the appropriate command or button to send the document to the printer. Next, open the window for the printer connected to your system, and pause the current print job. Then return to the WordPad window, and open the document stored in the **Letter** file. Send this document to the printer. Activate your printer's window. Cancel the print job for the document stored in **Letter**, and resume printing the document stored in **Memo**. Close all open windows.

2. If your printer has more than one printer resolution, access the Default Document Properties dialog box for your printer. (Otherwise, skip this project.) Set the appropriate options for low resolution and/or draft print quality. Next, open the WordPad accessory program. Open the document stored in the **Letter** file. Select the appropriate command or button to send the image to the printer. After the image prints, return to the printer's Default Document Properties dialog box and set the appropriate options for high resolution and/or letter print quality. Return to the WordPad program, send the image stored in **Letter** to the printer again, and compare the two printed images. Describe briefly any differences between the two outputs. Close all open windows.

3. Access your printer's Default Document Properties dialog box, and select the Landscape option. Next, open the Paint accessory program, and open the image stored in the **Fence** file. Send the image to the printer. Close the Paint program, open the window for the printer connected to your system, and pause the current print job. Then return to the Default Document Properties dialog box for the printer, and reset the orientation to Portrait. Resume the printing of the image, and then close all the windows.

4. Open the window for your printer. Then open the Paint accessory. Quickly open and send to the printer at least three Paint images such as **Blutube, Cupid**, and **Star**. Next, activate your printer's window and delete the second and third print jobs before they are sent to the printer. Allow the first print job to print, and then close all the windows.

5. Create print samples for at least three fonts in addition to the ones you sampled in Lesson 7. Keep these printouts to begin a font sample booklet that you can refer to for future font choices.

If you are finished working, log off the computer.

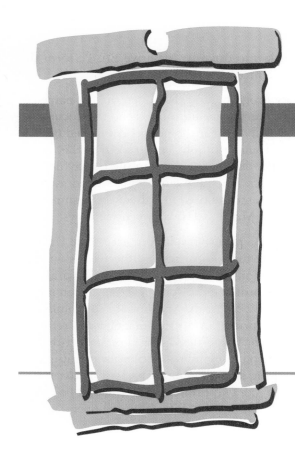

LESSON 8

COPYING, MOVING, EXCHANGING, AND SHARING DATA

OBJECTIVES

After you complete this lesson, you will be able to do the following:

- *Explain multitasking and how it facilitates data exchange.*

- *Describe the various ways that data can be copied, moved, and exchanged within and between files.*

- *Trace the development of data sharing methods from importing and exporting, to converting, linking, and object embedding.*

- *Drag-and-drop data from one document to another in WordPad.*

- *Place data into the Clipboard and view it.*

- *Use the Clipboard commands—Cut, Copy, Paste—to move and copy data within and between files and to move and copy files within and between disks.*

- *Use OLE to copy objects from one application to another and edit the objects without exiting the client application.*

n the early days of personal computers, combining data from two or more applications into one document was difficult or even impossible. Data created with different applications might be incompatible; and even when compatibility wasn't a problem, getting information out of one document and into another required creativity and tedious, time-consuming procedures.

The Windows interface makes combining objects from different applications much easier. Now with the release of Windows NT and Windows 95, users can take advantage of a new approach to data sharing—one that focuses specifically on the document and the tools used to create it.

Unlike the application focus of the past, personal computer users are entering a new era in which the availability of application "tools" adapts to the user's needs as the work product is being developed. In this lesson, you will learn how to use several techniques to combine objects into one document.

SHARING DATA

Before the development of graphical user interfaces, working on multiple documents required a user to go to exhaustive lengths. For instance, combining a graphic image with a text document required a user to open a word processing application; create, edit, and format the text in the application's proprietary format; save the text in a file; close the application; and then open the graphics application to create, edit, and save the image. Then the user needed to convert the data in the image file to a format that could be recognized by the word processing application, which of course had to be opened again. Different data formats often made it necessary to use a separate program to perform the data conversion.

MULTITASKING

In the early days of personal computers, users worked with one program and one document at a time. For example, if you were typing a letter using a word processing program and needed to check the balance on your checkbook, you saved your letter, quit the word processing program, started your financial management program, and reviewed your balance. To continue working on your letter, you quit the financial management program, started the word processing program, retrieved the letter from disk, and continued typing.

multitasking The ability of an operating system to carry out multiple operations at the same time; for example, running more than one program.

As hardware became more powerful, computers could handle more than one task or program at a time. Working with more than one program or file at a time is called **multitasking**. Now, when you want to review the balance of your checkbook, you don't have to save your document and quit your word processing program. You just "push" the letter aside on the Desktop, start the financial management program, view your balance, and resume working on your letter. Both the word processing program and the financial management program are running at the same time, each in its own window. You merely activate the window you want to use.

background The process of running a program while it is not on the screen.

Multitasking makes computing time-efficient. For instance, the computer can alphabetize a long list of names in the **background** or "invisibly" and still free up the screen so that you can open and use a different program to continue working. The print spooling that you used in Lesson 7 is another example of background processing.

application-centric approach A theoretical view of using computers that emphasizes proficiency with a program's interface. Compare with *document-centric approach*.

One advantage of multitasking is that you can combine different objects without having to open and close applications. However, despite that convenience, you must still learn the independent functions and features of each application. Working within different applications to create different types of data characterizes an **application-centric approach** to computing. With this approach, each application has its own user interface, and there is no guarantee of consistency from one program to another.

USING APPLICATION-CENTRIC SHARING METHODS

Four types of application-centric file-sharing methods exist: importing and exporting data, converting data, linking data, and sharing data within integrated software packages. You will take a closer look at each.

IMPORTING AND EXPORTING DATA

export To share data from an application by converting it to a format that can be read by another application.

import To share data created in another application by converting it to a format that can be displayed and modified in the current application.

Each application program saves files in its own unique format. For example, a database management program such as dBASE saves an address listing in a dBASE formatted file; Lotus 1-2-3, an electronic spreadsheet program, creates Lotus 1-2-3 worksheet files. The earliest method of moving data between programs involved saving information from one program in a format that another program could use. This is called **exporting**. When running the other program, the data could be retrieved from disk in a process known as **importing**. In this manner, the data from a database program could be incorporated into a spreadsheet program. This technique forced users to master both application programs.

CONVERTING DATA

To simplify data transfer, small translation programs were developed with the sole purpose of converting files from one format to another. Some sophisticated application software has conversion software built-in, so files can be converted from another format when the document is opened.

Once you import a graphic into a word processing document, the word processing program lacks the editing commands needed to make substantive changes to that graphic. Instead, to change the graphic, you need to open the original in the drawing program, edit it, and re-import the graphic into the word processing file. In a complex document, such as a newsletter with many illustrations, importing and re-importing graphics files can be very tedious and time-consuming.

LINKING DATA

linking Establishing a relationship between an object and the program that created it.

Dynamic Data Exchange (DDE) A data-sharing characteristic in which data modified in one application is also modified automatically in the application that shares the data.

Linking sets up an ongoing relationship between data and the program that created it, and eliminates the need to re-import the data every time it is edited. For example, editing a graphic could automatically update the graphic in the word processing file. This technique is sometimes called **Dynamic Data Exchange** (DDE). While this method provided an easier way to share information, the user still had to work with two application programs, one at a time.

USING INTEGRATED SOFTWARE PACKAGES

Integrated software packages combine features from several applications, such as word processing, spreadsheets, database, graphics, and communications, into one program. Microsoft Works, ClarisWorks, and Microsoft Office 97 are the best-selling software packages of this type. Having the same interface, these programs share different types of data relatively effortlessly. For home or personal use, these programs have deserved popularity. Unfortunately, none of them has the wealth of features or flexibility available in separate application programs.

USING WINDOWS NT DOCUMENT-CENTRIC METHODS

The developers of Windows NT realized that combining data created by different applications requires more than common user access, a graphical user interface, and multitasking. Instead, there must be a way to concentrate on the single document—the final product—without being overly concerned with the programs that create each type of information within the document. This view of computer work is called a **document-centric approach**.

document-centric approach A theoretical view of using computers that focuses on the document or product, rather than the application(s) used to create it, and emphasizes tools that adapt to users' needs. Compare with *application-centric approach*.

Data-sharing methods in Windows NT involve either dragging and dropping items from one location to another, or using the Windows NT Clipboard to hold data temporarily until it is deposited (copied or moved) to another location. Multiwindowing software such as Windows NT, provides a variety of methods for moving data between application programs. The first of these methods you have already experienced: drag-and-drop.

THE DRAG-AND-DROP PROCESS

This document-centric technique lets you drag an icon, a piece of a document, or an entire document to a new location to either move or duplicate that object. To drag and drop an object, you simply select it, drag it to its new location, and release the mouse button. Not all application programs allow you to drag from one window and drop into a window of another program.

SING THE CLIPBOARD

Clipboard A portion of random access memory (RAM) used to temporarily store information that has been cut or copied, so it can be pasted in a new location.

When you use the Cut or Copy commands in Windows NT, the selected information is placed in a special area of main memory called the **Clipboard**. The data in the Clipboard can be pasted elsewhere in the document window or in another document window, even if the second document window is in another application. If the programs support it, a link can be created to the software that placed the data in the Clipboard by using the Paste Link option on the Edit menu. Even if you cannot link the data, the Clipboard is an easy way to transfer information between any two applications—even between a Windows and a DOS program.

NOTE   *To edit linked data, use the Links option of the Edit menu.*

The data in the Clipboard can be either text or a graphic. If text, the data is stored in several formats. When you paste the text data, the computer chooses a generic format for the receiving application. At times, you can specify the text format. For example, if you copy text from a WordPad document, you can paste the text into another window as WordPad Document formatted, Formatted Text, or Unformatted Text.

A special Windows accessory program called Clipboard Viewer lets you examine the contents of the Clipboard. It helps you understand how the Clipboard commands work, and lets you save the contents of the Clipboard in a file for later use.

THE CLIPBOARD COMMANDS

Throughout Windows NT, each application's Edit menu has three consistent Clipboard commands: Cut, Copy, and Paste. These commands are used to duplicate or move data and files from one location to another.

Before you can copy or move something, you must select it. Copy places a replica of the selected object into the Clipboard and leaves the original alone. **Cut** places a replica of the selected object into the Clipboard and removes it from its original location.

cut An operation which removes any selected object, such as text, image, file, or folder, from its original location and stores it temporarily in the computer's memory; also the name of the command which performs this operation.

paste An operation which inserts an object temporarily stored in the computer's memory (the contents of the Windows Clipboard) at the currently active location; also the name of the command which performs this operation.

Executing the Cut or the Copy command is only half of the sequence required to move or duplicate an object. The Paste command finishes the process. **Paste** inserts the contents of the Clipboard at the currently active location, such as the insertion point in a text file or the Contents pane in the Exploring window. Thus Copy and Paste duplicates an object, while Cut and Paste moves it.

To use the Clipboard effectively, you should understand some of its restrictions. The Clipboard only holds its contents temporarily, as long as the computer is running. The Clipboard can only hold one object at a time, even though that object might be very large, such as a 15-page document. Each time that you Cut or Copy something, that object "bumps" or replaces the data previously stored there.

NOTE   *Make sure to paste any data you need before cutting or copying anything else into the Clipboard.*

ClipBook An area of disk storage that holds pages of information copied from other users' Clipboards. Pages in the ClipBook can be shared with other users on the network. See *Clipboard*.

Every Windows NT computer also has a **ClipBook.** You use the ClipBook to store data from the Clipboard and to share that information with other users on your network. Unlike the Clipboard, which holds only one piece of information at a time, the ClipBook can save many pieces of information. Each piece of information is saved on a separate "page." Pages in the ClipBook can be copied into the Clipboard and pasted into documents. You can also copy pages from other users' ClipBooks into your Clipboard.

COPYING DATA TO THE CLIPBOARD

In the following steps, you will copy data from a document into the Clipboard.

1. Open WordPad.

 2. Click the Open button on the WordPad toolbar.

3. Select the location in the Look In drop-down list for the drive that contains your Student Data Disk (drive A: or B:).

4. Select the Text Documents (*.txt) option on the Files Of Type list.

5. Double-click the **Expenses** file icon.

The data stored in text format appears in the WordPad window.

6. Choose Select All from the Edit menu to select all of the text in the document.

The entire document highlights.

7. Choose Copy from the Edit menu.

The selected text is copied to the Windows NT Clipboard.

VIEWING THE CONTENTS OF THE CLIPBOARD

In the following steps, you will see the information that you just copied into the Clipboard.

1. Choose Programs and then Accessories from the Start menu.

2. Click the Clipboard Viewer from the Accessories menu.

The ClipBook Viewer window appears, as shown in Figure 8-1.

3. Click the Window menu and then click the Clipboard option.

The data you copied from WordPad shows in the Clipboard.

4. Tile the open windows horizontally.

Your screen should resemble Figure 8-2.

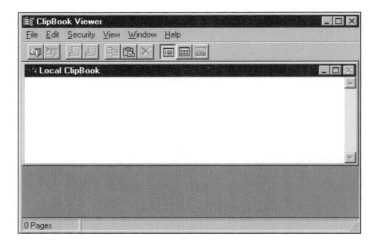

FIGURE 8-1

The ClipBook Viewer

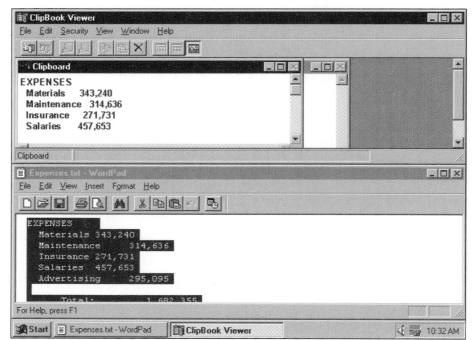

FIGURE 8-2

The tiled ClipBook Viewer and WordPad windows

PASTING BETWEEN DOCUMENTS

In the following steps, you will paste the data you copied into a different document.

HANDS ON

1. Click the WordPad's Open button.

The Open dialog box appears.

2. Make sure the disk location is set for the drive that contains your Student Data Disk.

3. Change the Files Of Type setting to All Documents.

4. Double-click the **Memo** icon.

The file opens and the document appears in the WordPad window.

5. Maximize the WordPad window.

6. Move the insertion point to the line below *tomorrow* near the end of the document.

7. Choose Paste from the Edit menu.

The copied text is pasted into the document at the insertion point. Notice that the text has the same formatting as in the original document (Courier New).

8. Click the Save button.

The changes to the file are saved.

9. Print the expanded document, if desired.

10. Restore the WordPad window so that you can see the ClipBook Viewer.

The ClipBook Viewer still contains the copied passage. It will do so until another object is cut or copied, or the computer is turned off.

11. Close the ClipBook Viewer.

DUPLICATING AND MOVING FILES WITH THE CLIPBOARD

Just as you can use the Clipboard commands to duplicate and move text, you can also use these commands to duplicate and move files. This method allows you to "hold" the data you're moving in memory until you are ready to place it in its new location.

To move a folder in the Exploring window from one location to another, you begin by highlighting the folder you want to move, and choosing Cut from the Edit menu. To complete the move operation, you open the folder where you want to place the folder you're moving, and choose Paste from the Exploring window's Edit menu.

NOTE *Whenever you select information, such as text or an icon, and then use the Cut or Copy command, the selected information is temporarily stored in the Clipboard. The information remains in the Clipboard until the next information you cut or copy replaces it. You can paste this information over and over again, so you could create as many copies, in as many different locations, as you like.*

The Copy and Paste commands work similarly, except that the file or folder remains in its original location with a duplicate placed first into the Clipboard (Copy) and then into the new location (Paste).

NOTE *If you want to move the file or files to another drive, you can cut and paste. Dragging files between different drives always copies them. Drag with the right mouse button to move them.*

USING OBJECT LINKING AND EMBEDDING

embedding A data-sharing method that involves integrating an object from one application into another.

By far, the most flexible and document-centric method of sharing data involves **embedding** (or integrating) an object, such as an image or a block of text, from one program into another program. The program responsible for creating or editing the object is called the **server**. The program that will contain the embedded object is called the **client**.

server The application responsible for creating or editing an object shared by two or more applications.

client In OLE technology, a program that receives an embedded object which was produced in another program. See *Object Linking and Embedding*.

Object Linking and Embedding (OLE) A data-sharing technology in which data created in one application is integrated into another application, and editing tools are available regardless of which application contains the embedded object.

Several standards exist for embedding objects between server and client applications—**Object Linking and Embedding (OLE)** and **OpenDoc**. In this lesson, you will use OLE, but OpenDoc compatibility works similarly.

To use OLE, both the client and server programs must support OLE. Here's how you embed an object from one program in the document of another program. First you use the server application to create the object. Then you select and save the object to disk. Next, you open the destination document in the client application. You use the Insert New Object command on the Insert menu to open a dialog box like the one shown in Figure 8-3. To select the object saved on disk, you can either click the Create From File button and enter the file name or browse through the disk contents to find the file, and then double-click it.

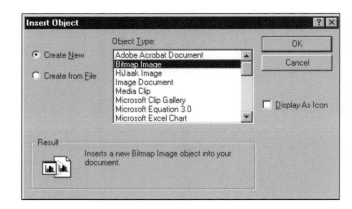

FIGURE 8-3
The Insert Object dialog box

OpenDoc A data-sharing technique similar to OLE.

In the most recent version, OLE 2.0, you can edit an embedded object right in the client application. Double-clicking the object brings the server application's menu, icons, and other editing aids into the client application window. The File and Windows menus belong to the client, while the other menus come from the server. When you click outside the object, your client application menus and toolbars return to normal.

NOTE

If both applications support it, you can use drag-and-drop to move an object from the server to the client window. While Windows NT 4.0 supports OLE 2.0, not all application software on your computer supports the latest standard. Therefore, you may find yourself limited to the older OLE 1.0 standard in which you edit an object in the server program; when you double-click the object in the client program, the server program opens.

COPYING AN OBJECT

In the following steps, you will open the Paint accessory program and copy an object to the Windows NT Clipboard.

NOTE

The steps to embedding an editable object into a document are the same as plain ordinary Copy and Paste. With OLE, however, the embedded object is editable, as you will see later.

HANDS ON

1. Make sure the WordPad window is open and visible on your Desktop.

2. Open the **Poem** file on your Student Data Disk.

3. Click the Start button on the taskbar.

4. Highlight Programs, and then highlight Accessories.

5. Select Paint.

   The Paint window opens and appears on the Desktop.

6. Maximize the Paint window, if necessary.

7. Open the image stored in the **Star** file on your Student Data Disk.

8. Click the Select tool, and drag a selection outline around the star image.

9. Choose Copy from the Edit menu.

   The selected image is copied to the Windows NT Clipboard.

10. Close the Paint window.

   Paint and the **Star** document are no longer in the computer's main memory.

EMBEDDING AN OBJECT

In the following steps, you will embed the copied bitmap object in a WordPad document.

HANDS ON

1. Activate and maximize the WordPad window, if necessary.

2. Press Ctrl+End to move the insertion point to the end of the document.

3. Choose Paste from the Edit menu.

   The image copied from the **Star** file appears in the document. Notice the frame surrounding the graphic and the square handles at each corner and midpoint of the frame. These features indicate that this graphic is an embedded object.

4. Click outside the frame.

   Your document should look similar to Figure 8-4. The pointer becomes an I-beam and the document has a blinking insertion point in the vicinity of where you clicked.

5. Click the star.

   Its frame and handles reappear to indicate that it is selected. The document does not display an insertion point.

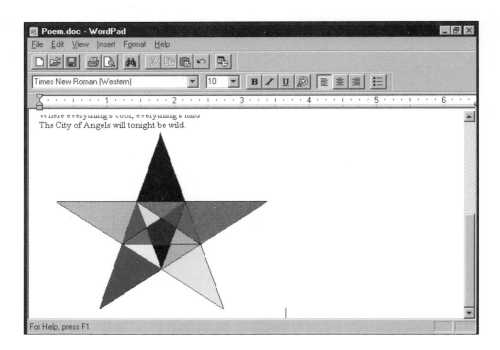

FIGURE 8-4

The embedded object in a WordPad document

6. Double-click inside the frame and wait while the Paint tools appear, as shown in Figure 8-5.

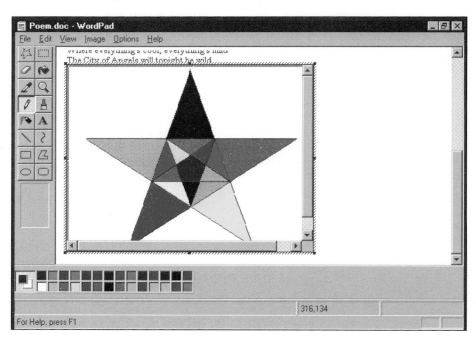

FIGURE 8-5

The embedded graphic with Paint tools in the WordPad document

Notice that the document's title bar still says "WordPad" and that the taskbar does not contain a Paint button. Paint is now open strictly inside of WordPad.

7. Select the Airbrush tool, click a light color from the palette and decorate the edges of the star, as shown in Figure 8-6.

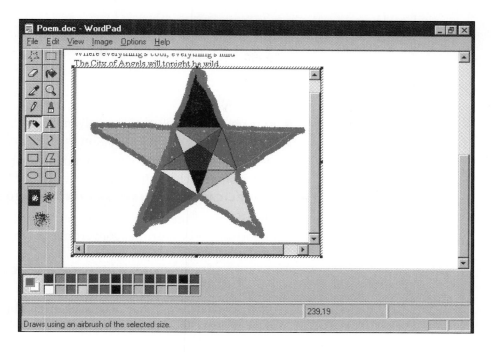

FIGURE 8-6

Editing the embedded graphic

8. Click to the right of the Paint frame.

The frame and the Paint tools vanish. The edited star appears in the WordPad document, with WordPad tools available.

9. Choose Save As from the File menu to save the file under a new name.

10. When the Save As dialog box appears, make sure the disk location is correct for the location of your Student Data Disk (drive A: or B:).

11. Activate the File Name text box, type **Winstar,** and click OK.

The document, containing the text from **Poem** and the image from **Star,** is saved in the new **Winstar** file on your Student Data Disk.

12. Click the Print button on the toolbar.

The document is sent to the printer and begins printing.

13. Close the WordPad window.

14. If you want to quit your work on the computer, log off your computer. Otherwise, leave your computer in its current status, and complete the exercises for this lesson.

ESSON SUMMARY AND EXERCISES

After you complete this lesson, you should know how to do the following:

SHARING DATA

- Explain the definition and advantages of multitasking and what it means for a program to work in the background.

- Describe the difference between a document-centric and an application-centric approach to sharing data.

USING APPLICATION-CENTRIC SHARING METHODS

- Identify the four types of sharing methods before OLE standards—importing and exporting, converting, linking, and using integrated software packages.

USING WINDOWS NT DOCUMENT–CENTRIC METHODS

- Drag-and-drop data between documents by selecting the object, holding down the left mouse button, moving the object to the desired location, and releasing the button. Use Ctrl with the mouse to copy rather than move the object.

USING THE CLIPBOARD

- Move text or graphics from one window to another by selecting the object, choosing Edit, and then choosing Cut. Then Edit and Paste in the other document. As a keyboard shortcut, to Cut, use Ctrl+x, and to Paste, use Ctrl+v.

- Copy text or graphics from one window to another by selecting the object, choosing Edit, and then choosing Copy. Then Edit and Paste in the other document. As a keyboard shortcut, to Copy, use Ctrl+c, and to Paste, use Ctrl+v.

- View, modify, or print the contents of the Clipboard by using WordPad for text or graphics, and using Paint for graphics.

USING OBJECT LINKING AND EMBEDDING

- Edit an object created by another program by double-clicking the object. If both programs use OLE 1.0, the other program will be run. If both programs use OLE 2.0, the other program's editing tools will be available to you.

NEW TERMS TO REMEMBER

After you complete this lesson, you should know the meaning of these terms:

application-centric approach	document-centric approach	linking
background		multitasking
client	Dynamic Data Exchange (DDE)	Object Linking and Embedding (OLE)
Clipboard	embedding	OpenDoc
ClipBook	export	paste
cut	import	server

MATCHING EXERCISE

Match each of the terms with the definitions on the right:

TERMS	DEFINITIONS
1. client	**a.** Establishing a relationship between an object and the application used originally to create the object
2. document-centricity	**b.** To save data in a format that is compatible with the type of data used by another application
3. Dynamic Data Exchange (DDE)	**c.** Rapidly evolving standard for application integration in which an object's server application tools become available when working with the object within the client application
4. embedding	
5. export	
6. import	
7. linking	**d.** Data-sharing component for an application that contains an embedded object
8. Object Linking and Embedding (OLE)	**e.** Linking technique for applications that allows data to be moved from one application to another and in which changes made in one application are reflected automatically in the other
9. background	
10. server	**f.** To insert data saved in a compatible format that was originally generated in another application
	g. Concept of working with computer data that is based on the document and not the applications used to create it
	h. Data-sharing component for the application used originally to create an object
	i. Inserting data generated within one application into a document generated by another application, thereby establishing a link
	j. Computer processing "behind the scenes" or other than in the active window

COMPLETION EXERCISE

Fill in the missing word or phrase for each of the following:

1. To the user, the concept of *document-centricity* means focusing more on developing and editing _____, with less emphasis on the _____ used to create it.

2. When you save data in a format that is compatible with another application, you are _____ the data.

3. A data *link* refers to a relationship between a(n) _____ and the _____ used to create it.

4. Using the mouse to physically move or copy data from an application in one window to an application in another is accomplished through the _____ technique.

5. The Windows NT _____ is a special area set aside within the computer's main memory to store data temporarily that is to be copied or moved.

6. Choose the _____ command if you wish to duplicate a selection to memory without removing the original from its current location.

7. The _____ application contains an embedded object that was created in the _____ application.

8. When you double-click an OLE 2.0 embedded object, the available menus and tools become those of the _____ application.

9. Inserting a table from a spreadsheet that was saved in text format into a document within a word processor is an example of _____ data.

10. One benefit of a(n) _____ operating system, such as Windows NT, is the ability to establish dynamic links between multiple applications.

SHORT-ANSWER QUESTIONS

Write a brief answer to each of the following questions:

1. Distinguish between exporting and importing data.

2. List and describe briefly two methods in which you can move or copy data between two different applications within the Windows NT environment.

3. Describe briefly the main difference between Dynamic Data Exchange (DDE) and Object Linking and Embedding (OLE), in terms of the user's ability to link data.

4. List three specific examples of how a compound document might be created employing the Object Linking and Embedding (OLE) technology.

5. Give one advantage and one disadvantage of using integrated software packages.

6. Distinguish between the Edit menu's Cut and Copy commands. Which one would you use to move a folder from one disk to another and why?

7. What is the purpose of the Clipboard, how do you see its contents, and what are some of its limitations?

8. What is multitasking? List three ways that you think multitasking might speed up your personal computing work.

9. Describe the process of embedding part of a Paint document into a text file. Use the terms *client* and *server* in your explanation.

10. Why does data sometimes fail to convert from one program to another?

APPLICATION PROJECTS

Insert your untitled disk into drive A: (or drive B:). Perform the following actions to complete these projects:

1. Open the WordPad accessory program. In a new document, list and define the methods of data sharing discussed in this lesson. Save the document in a new file named **DataShare** in the **Documents** folder on your Untitled Disk, and then print the document. Close all open windows.

2. Open a new WordPad document and type the following text:

Gill's Fencing
Repairs and New Installations
All Work Guaranteed
Reasonable Rates
(505) 555–6942

Next, open the My Computer or Explorer window and select the device icon for the drive that contains your Untitled Disk (drive A: or B:). Drag the icon labeled **Fence** to the end of the document in the WordPad window. Make any other editing changes to the document to suit your taste. For example, consider changing the text's font (and size), applying the bold attribute to the text, and centering the text. Save the document in a file named **FenceAd** in the **Documents** folder on your Untitled Disk. Print the document and then close the WordPad window.

3. Open the Paint accessory program. Use the Paint tools to design a graphic about 4 inches wide and 1 inch high that you can use to create personal stationery. Save the document as **My Logo1** on your Untitled Disk. Copy only the design part of the document and close the Paint window. Open a new WordPad document and paste the design at the top of the page. Click to the right of the graphic frame, press ⌷Enter⌷ to start a new line, type your name, press ⌷Enter⌷, and then type your address. Save this file as **My Stationery**. Print the document.

4. Open **My Stationery** if it is not already open and save it as **Letter to My Instructor** on your Untitled Disk. Use the stationery copy to write a letter to your instructor explaining what you do and do not like about your class. Save the document again and print your letter.

5. With your Student Data Disk inserted, open the Explorer window and acitvate the icon of the appropriate floppy disk. If you did not do Application Project 1 in Lesson 5, make two folders called **Graphics** and **WP-files**. Use Cut and Paste to move appropriate files from the root directory of the Student Data Disk into these folders.

When you are finished working, close all open windows and log off the computer.

COMMAND	DESCRIPTION	ICON
START BUTTON SHORTCUT MENU		
Open	Opens a Start Menu window	
Explore	Opens the Windows NT Explorer program	
Find	Opens the Find: All Files dialog box for setting options to locate files or folders	
TASKBAR SHORTCUT MENU		
Adjust Date/Time	Opens a dialog box for changing the system's time zone, date, and time settings (appears only when the mouse pointer is over the clock indicator)	
Cascade	Arranges all open windows on the Desktop so that they appear equally sized and stacked so that a small part of each inactive window is visible behind the active window	
Tile Windows Horizontally	Arranges all open windows on the Desktop so that they appear equally sized and occupy an equal horizontal portion of the Desktop	
Tile Windows Vertically	Arranges all open windows on the Desktop so that they appear equally sized and occupy an equal vertical portion of the Desktop	
Minimize All Windows	Reduces all open windows to buttons on the taskbar	
(Undo Minimize All)	Restores all windows minimized with the Minimize All Windows command	
Properties	Opens the Taskbar Properties dialog box for changing taskbar options	
DESKTOP SHORTCUT MENU		
Arrange Icons	Displays another pop-up menu of options for arranging Desktop icons by name, type, size, date, or automatically	
Line Up Icons	Aligns Desktop icons vertically from the left side of the Desktop to the right	
New	Displays another pop-up menu of options for creating new Desktop shortcut icons, folders, or other document icons corresponding to specific applications	

COMMAND	DESCRIPTION	ICON
Properties	Opens the Display Properties dialog box	

DEVICE ICON SHORTCUT MENU
This menu may contain additional items, depending on the device type.

Open	Opens the selected icon's window	
Explore	Opens the Exploring window	
Find	Opens the Find: All Files dialog box for setting options to locate files or folders	
Create Shortcut	Creates a shortcut icon for the selected object	
Properties	Displays the System Properties dialog box for changing a variety of system settings	

TASKBAR

START BUTTON

Programs	Displays another menu of group folders and Windows NT programs	
Documents	Displays a list of the most recently used documents	
Settings	Displays another menu of group folders	
Find	Opens the Find: All Files dialog box for setting options to locate files or folders	
Help	Displays the Help Topics: Windows NT Help dialog box for looking up Help information	
Run	Displays the Run dialog box for entering a line command to open a folder or program	
Shut Down	Initiates the process for shutting down or rebooting the operating system or logging on as a different user	

PROGRAMS MENU
This menu may contain additional submenus or commands, depending on your system's configuration.

Accessories	Displays submenu of accessory program names	
Command Prompt	Displays an MS-DOS Prompt window, which provides the MS-DOS command-line interface	
Windows NT Explorer	Opens the Exploring window, which provides disk and file management features	

ACCESSORIES MENU

Multimedia	Displays submenu of programs for playing sound, animation, or video on computers equipped with CD-ROM drives and sound cards	
System Tools	Displays submenu of programs that provide advanced system management and maintenance features	

COMMAND	DESCRIPTION	ICON
SETTINGS MENU		
Control Panel	Opens the Control Panel window, which provides access to a variety of system management programs	
Printers	Opens the Printers window, which provides access to print queue windows for installed printers and a program for installing a printer	
Taskbar	Opens the Taskbar Properties dialog box for controlling taskbar options	
CONTROL PANEL WINDOW		
Accessibility Options	Changes accessibility options for your system	Accessibility Options
Add/Remove Programs	Opens wizard for installing or uninstalling programs	Add/Remove Programs
Date/Time	Opens the Date/Time Properties dialog box	Date/Time
Display	Opens the Display Properties dialog box	Display
Fonts	Opens the Fonts (folder) window	Fonts
Keyboard	Opens the Keyboard Properties dialog box	Keyboard
Modems	Opens a dialog box for changing modem settings	Modems
Mouse	Opens the Mouse Properties dialog box	Mouse
Multimedia	Opens a dialog box for changing video and sound settings	Multimedia
Printers	Opens the Printers window	Printers
Sounds	Opens a dialog box for changing sound board settings	Sounds

COMMAND	DESCRIPTION	ICON
System	Opens the System Properties dialog box	System

FIND MENU

Files or Folders	Opens the Find: All Files dialog box for setting options to locate files or folders	

OPTIONAL ACCESSORIES MENU COMMANDS

This menu may contain additional items, depending on your system's configuration.

Calculator	Opens a program that provides a standard or scientific calculator	
Clipboard Viewer	Opens a window that provides a view of the current contents in the Windows NT Clipboard	
Notepad	Opens a program window for creating and editing unformatted text documents.	
Paint	Opens a program window that provides tools for creating graphic objects	
WordPad	Opens a program window for creating, editing, formatting, and printing text documents	

DEVICE WINDOWS

This menu may contain additional items, depending on the device type.

FILE MENU

Create Shortcut	Creates a shortcut icon for the selected object
Delete	Deletes the selected object and places it in the Recycle Bin
Rename	Highlights the selected object's name so that it can be edited
Properties	Displays the System Properties dialog box for changing a variety of system settings
Close	Closes the active device window

EDIT MENU

Undo	Undoes (reverses) the last operation
Cut	Cuts (removes) the selected object to the Windows NT Clipboard
Copy	Copies (duplicates) the selected object, placing the copy in the Windows NT Clipboard
Paste	Pastes (places) a previously cut or copied object from the Windows NT Clipboard into the selected location
Paste Shortcut	Pastes (places) a previously cut or copied object from the Windows NT Clipboard into the selected location as a shortcut icon

COMMAND	DESCRIPTION	ICON
Select All	Selects (highlights) all objects in the active window	
Invert Selection	Selects (highlights) unselected objects and deselects (removes highlighting from) selected objects	

VIEW MENU

COMMAND	DESCRIPTION	ICON
Toolbar	Toggles the display of the window's toolbar	
Status Bar	Toggles the display of the window's status bar	
Large Icons	Changes the display of the window's objects to large icons	
Small Icons	Changes the display of the window's objects to small icons	
List	Changes the display of the window's objects to small icons, which are listed line by line	
Details	Changes the display of the window's objects to small icons, and a columnar list of the files' names, types, size, and creation dates and times	
Arrange Icons	Displays a pop-up menu that arranges the window's objects by name, date, type, size, or automatically when the window is sized	
Line up Icons	Aligns a window's objects vertically from left to right	
Refresh	Updates the information displayed in the window to reflect the most current changes	
Options	Opens a dialog box for changing view options	

HELP MENU

COMMAND	DESCRIPTION	ICON
Help Topics	Opens the Help Topics: Windows NT Help dialog box for displaying help information	
About Windows NT	Displays information about who the system's version of Windows NT is licensed to and the current status of system resources	

EXPLORING WINDOW MENU BAR

FILE MENU

COMMAND	DESCRIPTION	ICON
New	Creates a new folder object in the selected folder or storage device	
Create Shortcut	Creates a shortcut icon for a selected program or object	
Delete	Deletes (removes) selected objects to the Recycle Bin	
Rename	Highlights the selected object's name so that it can be edited	

COMMAND	DESCRIPTION	ICON
Properties	Opens a Properties dialog box for the selected object	
Close	Closes the Exploring window	
EDIT MENU		
Undo	Reverses the last operation performed with Windows NT Explorer	
Cut	Cuts (removes) a selected object to the Windows NT Clipboard	
Copy	Copies (duplicates) a selected object and places the copy in the Windows NT clipboard	
Paste	Pastes (places) a previously cut or copied object from the Windows NT Clipboard into a new location	
Paste Shortcut	Creates a shortcut icon for a selected object	
Select All	Selects (highlights) all objects in the active folder	
Invert Selection	Selects (highlights) unselected objects and deselects (removes highlighting from) selected objects	
VIEW MENU		
Toolbar	Toggles the display of the Exploring window's toolbar	
Status Bar	Toggles the display of the Exploring window's status bar	
Large Icons	Changes the display of objects in the Contents pane to large icons	
Small Icons	Changes the display of objects in the Contents pane to small icons	
List	Changes the display of objects in the Contents pane to small icons and lists them line by line	
Details	Changes the display of objects in the Contents pane to small icons and lists them, line by line, with their type, size, and creation date and time information	
Arrange Icons	Arranges objects by name, type, size, date, or automatically as the Exploring window is sized	
Line up Icons	Aligns objects vertically from left to right in the Contents pane	
Refresh	Updates the display of the Exploring window to reflect the most recent changes	
Options	Opens a dialog box so that View options can be changed	

COMMAND	DESCRIPTION	ICON
TOOLS MENU		
Find	Opens the Find: All Files dialog box for changing options to locate files or folders	
Go To	Displays a dialog box for moving straight to a specific folder	
HELP MENU		
Help Topics	Opens the Help Topics: Windows NT Help dialog box for displaying help information	
About Windows NT	Displays information about who the system's version of Windows NT is licensed to and the current status of system resources	
CALCULATOR ACCESSORY PROGRAM MENU BAR		
EDIT MENU		
Copy	Copies the current value on the calculator's display to the Windows NT Clipboard	
Paste	Pastes (inserts) a value from the Windows NT Clipboard into the calculator's display	
VIEW MENU		
Scientific	Expands the calculator's appearance to provide scientific functions	
Standard	Reduces the calculator's appearance to display standard calculator features	
HELP MENU		
Help Topics	Opens the Help Topics: Calculator Help dialog box for displaying help information	
About Calculator	Displays information about who the system's version of Windows NT is licensed to and the current status of system resources	
PAINT ACCESSORY PROGRAM MENU BAR		
FILE MENU		
New	Opens a new, blank, and untitled image area	
Open	Opens an existing image file for editing	
Save	Stores the current changes to the active image file or displays the Save As dialog box on a first-time save	
Save As	Displays the Save As dialog box so that a previously unsaved image can be named and saved or an existing file can be saved under a different name	
Print Preview	Opens a print preview window that displays a facsimile of how the image will appear when printed	
Page Setup	Opens a dialog box for changing page settings for the active image file	

COMMAND	DESCRIPTION	ICON
Print	Opens a dialog box for selecting options and sending the active image data to the default printer	
Set As Wallpaper (Tiled)	Tiles this bitmap as the Desktop wallpaper	
Set As Wallpaper (Centered)	Centers this bitmap as the Desktop wallpaper	
Send	Transfers the image to another computer (network only)	
Exit	Closes the Paint window (program)	

EDIT MENU

Undo	Reverses the last editing operation	
Repeat	Repeats the last editing operation	
Cut	Cuts a selected portion of the image to the Windows NT Clipboard	
Copy	Copies a selected portion of the image to the Windows NT Clipboard	
Paste	Pastes the contents of the Windows NT Clipboard into the image	
Clear Selection	Removes the selection marker from a selected portion of the image	
Select All	Selects all objects or elements in the image	
Copy To	Copies a selected portion of the image to another file	
Paste From	Imports an object from another file into the active image file	

VIEW MENU

Tool Box	Toggles the display of the tool box	
Color Box	Toggles the display of the color box	
Status Bar	Toggles the display of the status bar	
Zoom	Modifies the display size of the image	
View Bitmap	Displays the active image temporarily in full-screen size	
Text Toolbar	Toggles the display of a toolbar for text editing	

IMAGE MENU

Flip/Rotate	Displays a dialog box for flipping or rotating a selected portion of an image vertically, horizontally, or by varying degrees about an axis	

COMMAND	DESCRIPTION	ICON
Stretch/Skew	Displays a dialog box for stretching or skewing a selected portion of an image by varying degrees vertically or horizontally	
Invert Colors	Changes the current colors for a selected portion of an image	
Attributes	Displays a dialog box for changing size attributes for the current image	
Clear Image	Clears the image editing area	

OPTIONS MENU

Edit Colors	Displays a dialog box for modifying existing colors or creating new colors	
Get Colors	Opens a file with a stored Color Box palette	
Save Colors	Saves the current Color Box palette in a file	
Draw Opaque	Toggles the transparency/opaque characteristic of selected portions of an image	

HELP MENU

Help Topics	Opens the Help Topics: Paint Help dialog box for displaying help information	
About Paint	Displays the Paint icon, name, version number, and other information	

WORDPAD ACCESSORY PROGRAM MENU BAR

FILE MENU

New	Opens a new, blank, and untitled document	🗋
Open	Opens an existing document file for editing	📂
Save	Stores the current changes to the active document file or displays the Save As dialog box on a first-time save	💾
Save As	Displays the Save As dialog box so that a previously unsaved document can be named and saved or an existing file can be saved under a different name	
Print	Opens a dialog box for selecting options and sending the active document's data to the default printer	🖨
Print Preview	Opens a print preview window that displays a facsimile of how the document will appear when printed	🔍
Page Setup	Opens a dialog box for changing page settings for the active document file	
Send	Transfers the document to another computer	

COMMAND	DESCRIPTION	ICON
Exit	Closes the WordPad window (program)	
EDIT MENU		
Undo	Reverses the last editing operation	
Cut	Cuts selected text to the Windows NT Clipboard	
Copy	Copies selected text to the Windows NT Clipboard	
Paste	Pastes the contents of the Windows NT Clipboard into the document	
Paste Special	Inserts the contents of the Windows NT Clipboard with options	
Paste Link	Inserts the contents of the Windows NT Clipboard along with a link to the data's source application	
Clear	Erases (deletes) selected text	
Select All	Selects (highlights) all the text in the document	
Find	Displays a dialog box for finding a specific text string in a document	
Find Next	Repeats the last Find operation	
Replace	Finds all or selected occurrences of a specified text string and replaces it with a specified text string	
Links	Provides for editing of linked objects	
Object Properties	Provides for changing the properties of a linked object	
Object	Activates a linked object for editing	
VIEW MENU		
Toolbar	Toggles the display of the WordPad window's Standard toolbar	
Format Bar	Toggles the display of the WordPad window's format bar	
Ruler	Toggles the display of the WordPad window's ruler	
Status Bar	Toggles the display of the WordPad window's status bar	
Options	Displays the Options dialog box for setting WordPad window view options	
INSERT MENU		
Date and Time	Inserts the current date and/or time into a document	
Object	Inserts a new embedded object in the active document	

COMMAND	DESCRIPTION	ICON
FORMAT MENU		
Font	Displays a dialog box for changing selected text's font settings	
Bullet Style	Formats selected paragraphs with hanging indents and bullet characters	
Paragraph	Provides for changing selected paragraph's indentation and alignment	
Tabs	Provides for changing selected paragraph's tab stop settings	
HELP MENU		
Help Topics	Opens the Help Topics: Windows NT Help dialog box for displaying help information	
About WordPad	Displays the WordPad icon, name, and other information	

accessories (or applets) Operating system programs or third-party software that supplement Windows NT 4.0 with application features, such as editing, drawing, and communications.

active window The window ready to accept input from the mouse or keyboard, indicated by a colored title bar; only one open window is active.

applets See *accessories*.

application file See *program file*.

application Specialized software program for accomplishing a specific task, such as creating text, manipulating financial information, or keeping track of records.

application window A rectangle on the Desktop containing an application's menus and documents.

application-centric approach A theoretical view of using computers that emphasizes proficiency with a program's interface. Compare with *document-centric approach*.

application-oriented structure A file management system in which subfolders within an application's folder are used to store data files created with the application. Compare with *project-oriented structure*.

attribute Enhancement or stylistic characteristic applied to text characters in a font, for example, bold, italic, and underlining.

backbone Computers that make up the Internet.

background The process of running a program while it is not on the screen.

back up (v.) To copy (and/or compress) data for storage elsewhere in case it is needed to restore damaged or lost original data.

backup (n.) A copied and/or compressed set of data from which damaged or lost original data can be restored.

bitmap font (or nonscaleable font) A typeface in which each character is composed of a dot pattern that dictates the shape and size of the font.

booting the system Another expression for starting up, which the computer often accomplishes by loading a small program, which then reads a larger program into memory.

browser A software package that lets the user access the major components of the Internet, such as the World Wide Web, e-mail, and so on.

button A box labeled with words or pictures that can be clicked to select a setting or put a command into effect.

cascade A technique for arranging open windows in equal size and stacked, so that only the top window is fully visible and the upper-left corners of the other windows appear behind it.

check box A square in a dialog box that contains a ✓ when an option is selected or appears empty when the option is not selected.

clicking The technique of quickly pressing and releasing the left button on a mouse or trackball.

client In OLE technology, a program that receives an embedded object which was produced in another program. See *Object Linking and Embedding*.

clients Individual computers within the network controlled by Windows NT.

Clipboard A portion of random access memory (RAM) used to temporarily store information that has been cut or copied, so it can be pasted in a new location.

ClipBook An area of disk storage that holds pages of information copied from other users' Clipboards. Pages in the ClipBook can be shared with other users on the network. See *Clipboard*.

close To remove a window from the screen.

collapsed   A state of an item in which details or subordinate items are hidden from view. A plus sign (+) in the box to the left of the item indicates the item is collapsed. Compare with *expanded*.

Color box (or palette)   A device at the bottom of the Paint window that contains a set of colors displayed in small squares, which can be selected to change a shape's color.

commands   Instructions that you issue to the computer, usually by choosing from a menu, clicking a button, or pressing a combination of keys on the keyboard.

command button   A rectangular control in a dialog box that carries out a specific task when clicked with a pointing device.

Contents pane   An area of the Exploring window that lists the contents of the disk or folder that is selected in the All Folders pane.

control menu icon   In Windows NT, a small control, typically on the left side of the title bar, that when clicked displays a menu for manipulating the window.

control panel   A dialog box that lets you change the settings on your computer.

copy   (1) An operation which temporarily stores a duplicate of any selected object, such as text, image, file, or folder, in the computer's memory; (2) the name of the command that performs this operation; (3) any object that duplicates an original and, in the case of files or folders, may or may not have the same name as the original, depending on the copy's location.

counter button   A control used to change a numerical setting, consisting of an up arrow above a down arrow; clicking the up arrow increases the setting; clicking the down arrow decreases it.

cut   An operation which removes any selected object, such as text, image, file, or folder, from its original location and stores it temporarily in the computer's memory; also the name of the command which performs this operation.

data   On a personal computer, information that is stored digitally and represents work a user creates or manipulates with the computer.

data file See *document file.*

default   A value or setting that software uses automatically unless you specify a different value or setting.

delete   An operation which removes any selected item, such as text, image, file, or folder, from a disk; in Windows NT the deleted item is sent to the Recycle Bin, which holds it until it is either restored to its original location or removed permanently.

deselect (deselected)   To return an object to its original color or turn off an option, indicating that an item will not be affected by the next action you take or that an option will no longer be in effect.

Desktop   The working area of the screen which displays many Windows NT tools and is the background for your computer work.

Desktop accessory   A small program built into the Windows NT operating system.

Detail view   An option for displaying objects in the Contents pane in the Exploring window, which shows the name, size, type, and date and time modified for each object in the Contents pane.

device   A piece of equipment (hardware), such as a printer or disk drive, that is part of your computer system.

device drivers Part of the Windows NT Executive Services that takes information from the I/O Manager and translates these instructions to operate the hardware device itself.

device icon   A small image that represents a hardware device, such as a printer or disk drive, installed on the computer system.

dialog box   A rectangle containing a set of options that appears when Windows NT needs more information from the user in order to perform a requested operation.

directory   An earlier term for *folder.*

disk structure   The organizational structure of folders and subfolders on a disk.

document files   Files that store the work you have done with the computer.

document window A rectangle within an application window for viewing and working on a document.

document-centric approach A theoretical view of using computers that focuses on the document or product, rather than the application(s) used to create it, and emphasizes tools that adapt to users' needs. Compare with *application-centric approach*.

DOS Acronym for *Disk Operating System*, a text-based, command-line operating system in widespread use on personal computers.

double-click The technique of rapidly pressing and releasing the button on a mouse or trackball twice when the mouse pointer on screen is pointing to an object.

draft Lowest resolution print quality setting, typically used for printing rough drafts rapidly.

drag-and-drop (or **dragging**) The technique of moving an object on screen by pointing to the object, pressing and holding the left mouse button, moving the mouse to the new location, and then releasing the button.

drive icon A small image that represents a storage device.

drop-down list A list of options displayed when you click a triangle button.

Dynamic Data Exchange (DDE) A data-sharing characteristic in which data modified in one application is also modified automatically in the application that shares the data.

e-mail Another name for electronic mail, information that is exchanged between two computers via telephone lines or network connections.

embedding A data-sharing method that involves integrating an object from one application into another.

expanded A state of an item in which details or subordinate items are visible. A minus sign (-) in the box to the left of the item indicates the item is expanded. Compare with *collapsed*.

export To share data from an application by converting it to a format that can be read by another application.

extension A one-to-three character file name component that is used to identify the type of data stored in the file.

file A named, ordered collection of information stored on a disk.

file allocation table (FAT) Disk file system that the operating system uses to read data from and write data to the disk. Used in Windows NT 4.0 to maintain compatibility with previous versions of Windows and DOS.

file icon A small image that represents a specific type of named data on screen.

file management The process of organizing and caring for your disks and files.

file name The characters used to identify a file, limited to 255 characters in Windows 95 and Windows NT 4.0 and 8 characters in DOS and older versions of Windows.

file-naming conventions The rules governing the length and character requirements for file names created within a specific operating system.

file system The method used by the operating system to control access to a disk.

Find An operation that attempts to locate: (1) a folder or file by identifying its network, disk drive, or folder; (2) specific content within a document by selecting and displaying it.

folder A named icon that contains files and other folders.

font A set of characters that appear with a specific typeface, one or more attributes, and a specific size.

format bar A row of buttons within a window, just below the toolbar, containing shortcuts for common formatting commands.

formatted file A document containing elements that enhance the appearance of text, paragraphs, and other objects, in order to make the document more attractive and understandable. Compare with *text file*.

formatting   (1) An operating system process which removes all existing data from a disk and prepares the disk to receive new data; (2) enhancements applied within a document to make the document more readable and attractive.

glossary term   In Windows NT Help windows, a word or phrase that appears underlined with dots and can be selected to display a definition.

graphical user interface (GUI)   An operating environment in which controls and data are visible on screen so they can be selected with a pointing device.

Graphics Device Interface (GDI)   Part of the Windows NT Executive Services that controls the display of graphics on the monitor and printers.

group folder   A special folder that includes a picture on its icon and which contains other program icons and/or device icons.

hard copy   Information that has been printed from its electronic, or "soft," form of storage on a computer, onto paper.

hardware   The parts of a computer system that you can see and touch.

Hardware Abstraction Layer (HAL)   Module in the kernel. Consists of system software instructions that communicate between the hardware and the rest of the operating system.

highlight (v.)   To change the color of an object to one that contrasts with its usual appearance.

home page   The main page of a World Wide Web site which usually includes links to other pages at that site.

horizontal scroll bar   A rectangular bar that appears along the bottom of a window that is too narrow to display all its contents; clicking or dragging in the scroll bar brings additional contents into view.

I/O Manager   Part of the Windows NT Executive Services that takes care of the flow of data into and out of the computer.

icon   A small image that represents a device, program, file, or folder.

import   To share data created in another application by converting it to a format that can be displayed and modified in the current application.

inactive window   Any window that will not accept mouse or keyboard input until it is made active; inactive windows have clear or gray title bars.

insertion point   A small blinking vertical line that indicates where the next character typed at the keyboard will appear on screen.

Internet   A collection of computers linked together into a huge network.

Internet service providers (or ISPs)   Companies that provide Internet access to users for a monthly or an annual fee.

jump   In Windows NT Help, a word or phrase that, when selected, immediately displays additional, related information.

kernel mode   A special means of operating the computer that can access any memory location, CPU function, or hardware resource. The Windows NT operating system runs in the kernel mode. Contrast with *user mode*.

keyword   Word or phrase used to define or narrow a search.

landscape orientation   A page layout option which prints text and graphics across the longer dimension of a page.

large icon   An icon displayed at full-size.

letter quality   Highest resolution print quality setting, typically used for printing final drafts.

linking   Establishing a relationship between an object and the program that created it.

links   Locations on a Web page that you click to jump to other locations or parts of the Internet.

log on   The process of identifying yourself to the computer system. Logging on determines how the user may interact with the system, including the resources to which the user has access. Users can also set up the user interface to match their own needs and preferences.

log off   Inform the operating system that the current user is no longer working on the computer.

main folder   The top level of a disk icon, which contains files and folders that are not nested within any other folder; also referred to as the root directory.

maximize   A Windows sizing feature in which an open window is enlarged to fill the screen; also, the name of the button which performs this function.

menu   A list of items on the screen from which you can choose; menu usually refers to a list of commands or options.

menu bar   An area below the title bar of all application windows containing the names of menus which, when clicked, displays a list of commands.

Microkernel   Module in the kernel. Handles the scheduling of multitasking programs and works closely with the HAL.

minimize   A Windows sizing feature which reduces an open window to a button on the taskbar; also, the name of the button which performs this function.

modem   Hardware that transfers data by converting computer signals that can be transmitted over a telephone line.

mouse pointer See *pointer*.

move   An operation in which a selected object is removed from its original location and placed elsewhere.

multitasking   The ability of an operating system to carry out multiple operations at the same time; for example, running more than one program.

multimedia   Documents or software which combine sound, text, graphics, animation, and/or video.

nonscalable font See *bitmap font*.

NT File System (NTFS) A file system new to Windows NT 4.0 that provides greater efficiency and security than the FAT file system.

NT Virtual DOS Machine (NTVDM) A process in which Windows NT 4.0 runs DOS-based programs. In an NTVDM, the application "thinks" it is running on a 486 machine under DOS.

Object Linking and Embedding (OLE)   A data-sharing technology in which data created in one application is integrated into another application, and editing tools are available regardless of which application contains the embedded object.

online services   Companies that include Internet access as a part of their own proprietary offerings.

on-screen Help   A window that opens to provide contextual assistance and other learning aids.

open   To access the contents of an icon in a window.

OpenDoc   A data-sharing technique similar to OLE.

operating system (software)   A collection of programs that allows you to work with a computer by managing the flow of data between input devices, the computer's memory, storage devices, and output devices.

option button   Small circle in a dialog box, also called a radio button, that is filled to indicate an option is selected or empty when not selected; only one in a set of option buttons can be selected at a time.

palette See *Color box*.

pane   A bordered area within a window.

parent folder   A folder that contains one or more folders (also called subfolders).

password   In Windows NT, a code (up to 14 characters) known only to the user. Having a secret password ensures that only authorized users can access the computer system.

paste   An operation which inserts an object temporarily stored in the computer's memory (the contents of the Windows NT Clipboard) at the currently active location; also the name of the command which performs this operation.

pixel   Short for picture element; the smallest dot you can draw on the screen and the smallest unit that images on the screen consist of.

point   (1) The action of pointing; (2) a unit of measurement equal to $\frac{1}{72}$ inch that is used to describe the height of type and other elements on a printed page.

pointer (or **mouse pointer**)   An arrow or other on-screen image that moves in relation to the movement of a mouse or trackball.

pointing   Moving the mouse pointer to position it over an on-screen object.

pop-up menu   A control which, when clicked, displays a list of commands or options.

portrait orientation   A page layout option in which text and graphics are printed across the shorter dimension of a page.

Power On Self Test (POST)   A program that checks a computer system's memory, keyboard, display, and disk drives.

print queue   Temporary storage area in memory or on disk for data sent to a printer; in Windows NT, the name for a window showing active print jobs.

print spooling   Process of sending print jobs to a print queue so that printing can take place while the computer is used for other tasks.

printer driver   A program that regulates the operation of a specific printer model and in Windows NT is represented by a device icon.

program files   Files that let you perform tasks on the computer.

project-oriented structure   A file management system in which data files and folders are organized according to the specific projects. Compare with *application-oriented structure*.

pull-down list   A control which normally displays a text box containing the selected item on a list and which, when clicked, displays the full list, so a different item can be selected.

pull-down menu   A list of commands that appears when the menu name on a window's menu bar is selected.

purging   Canceling all jobs in a print queue.

radio button   A small circle which is filled with a solid dot when the button is selected; only one in a set of radio buttons can be selected.

rename   To change the name of a file, a folder, or an icon.

resolution   A measurement of image quality usually applied to printers and computer monitors; printer resolution is typically expressed in dots per inch (dpi).

restore   (1) To return a maximized window to its previous size; also the name of the button that performs this function; (2) To return a deleted item to its original location, generally from the Recycle Bin.

root directory   An earlier name for the main folder in a disk.

ruler   A display of buttons and numbered tick marks beneath the WordPad format bar, which indicates measurements across the width of the document and is used to format paragraphs of text.

sans serif   A typeface whose characters lack extra lines at the ends of the strokes; sans serif typefaces are generally used for headings or display text.

scaleable font   Typeface that can be printed in a range of sizes.

screen capture   A graphical image of the computer screen display that is stored temporarily in the computer's memory, saved on disk, or printed.

scroll arrows   Buttons in a scroll bar that let you scroll information in a window in small increments—for example, scrolling text line by line.

scroll bar   A rectangular bar that appears along the right or bottom of a window when not all the window's contents are visible and which is used to bring the contents into view.

scroll box   A rectangle in a scroll bar that can be dragged to display information; its location represents the location of the visible information in relation to the window's entire contents.

search engine   A company that lists Web sites. The user enters a keyword and the search engine lists sites that most nearly match it.

select (v.)   To designate (typically by clicking an item with the mouse) where the next action will take place, which command will be executed next, or which option will be put into effect.

selected (adj.)   Term describing object(s) that will be affected by the next action or option(s) designated to go into effect.

separator line   A line dividing two panes in a window, which can be dragged to make one pane larger and the other smaller.

serif   An extra line at the end of a text character stroke that is part of the character design.

serif font   A typeface whose characters have extra lines at the ends of the strokes which make text more readable; serif typefaces are generally used for paragraph text.

server   The application responsible for creating or editing an object shared by two or more applications.

shared drive   A storage device that can be used by other users of the computer or network.

shared folder   A folder that can be used by other users of the computer or network.

shared printer   A printer that can be used by other users of the computer or network.

shortcut icon   A picture representing a quick path to a program or task.

shortcut menu   A list of an item's most frequently used commands.

size   To change the dimensions of a window so that its contents remain visible, but the window occupies only a portion of the Desktop.

small icon   An icon displayed at quarter size.

software   A collective term for programs, the instructions that are stored in electronic form and tell the computer what to do.

status bar   A bar at the bottom of a window that explains selected objects or menu commands.

subdirectory   An earlier term for a *subfolder*.

subfolder   A folder nested within another folder.

system   See *operating system*.

system boot   See *booting the system*.

system files   The files that operate the computer.

system icon   A picture representing an operating system file.

system properties   Settings that affect the overall operation of your computer and the devices connected to it.

taskbar   An area on the Windows NT Desktop which displays buttons for the Start menu, Clock, and any open windows.

text box   A rectangular control that displays the name or value of a current setting and in which you can type a different name or value to change the setting.

text editor   A program which creates text files.

text file (or **unformatted file**)   A data file containing text characters (letters, numbers, symbols, punctuation, spaces, and paragraph returns) without line, paragraph, or page formatting or typeface enhancements. Compare with *formatted file*.

tile   A technique for arranging open windows side by side and equally sized so that all are fully visible.

title bar   An area at the top of a window that displays the name of the application, document, or device which the window represents.

toggle   A command or an option that can be turned on and off by repeatedly clicking the command or option.

toolbar   (1) In WordPad, a row of buttons just below the menu bar containing shortcuts for common menu commands; (2) in Paint, a set of buttons at the left of the window, containing tools for creating an image.

tool box   An area in the Windows NT Paint accessory window containing icons representing the tools used to create an image.

Tool Tip   Text which appears when you point to a tool and provides information about the tool.

tree   A branching, hierarchical list that looks like the spreading branches or roots of a tree.

triangle button   A button in the shape of a small downward-pointing triangle, which displays a menu of options when clicked.

truncated An object that is cut off, for example, by a border, so that part of it is not displayed.

type (of icon/file) The category of information or application to which an icon or a file belongs.

typeface A specific design for a set of text characters which makes all the characters similar in appearance.

unformatted file See *text file*.

Universal Resource Locator (URL) Address of a Web site.

user interface A term for the rules and methods by which a computer and its users communicate.

user mode Applications run in this mode. In the user mode, programs can only address their own memory space. Contrast with *kernel mode*.

user name A unique name generally assigned to the user by the network administrator.

user-oriented structure A file management system in which data files and folders are organized according to the individual users who share a computer or network server.

vertical scroll bar A rectangular bar that appears along the right side of a window that is too short to display all its contents; clicking or dragging in the scroll bar brings additional contents into view.

video conferencing Exchanging audio and video conversations electronically.

virtual memory Hard disk space used by the operating system as if it were additional main memory.

Virtual Memory Manager Part of the Windows NT Executive Services that keeps track of memory usage by each running program.

Virtual–86 mode The processor mode that handles the execution of DOS program instructions under Windows NT.

Web pages Screens that display information on the Web. Many Web pages contain text, graphics, animation, sound, and video.

Web site Specific location of pages on the World Wide Web. A web site has an address, or URL.

weight An attribute applied to on-screen text or printed characters that influences the thickness of the characters and the spacing between them.

wildcard character Character that you can use in a Find operation to represent either a single unknown character or multiple consecutive characters (called strings).

window A rectangular area that displays information, such as the content of a document or the controls of an application; a window can be opened, closed, moved, sized, maximized, and minimized.

Window Manager Part of the Windows NT Executive Services that creates the screen interface that you see when you use Windows NT.

window pane A bordered area within a window.

wizard An automated process that guides you through an operation by presenting a series of options from which you can select.

word processor A software application designed for writing, editing, and enhancing the appearance of text.

word wrap A word processing feature that automatically breaks lines at the right margin or right side of a window as you type.

World Wide Web (or Web) Screens of graphical information on the Internet controlled by companies, organizations, and individuals with a special interest to share.

WOW (Win16 on Win32) A method by which Windows NT runs 16-bit Windows programs. The NTVDM can handle more than one 16-bit program at a time. Compare with *NT Virtual Dos Machine*.

WYSIWYG An acronym for What You See Is What You Get, a GUI characteristic in which documents appear on screen much as they will appear on a printed page.